GETTING ✓ IT RIGHT

Letter Writing

GETTING ✓ IT RIGHT

Letter Writing

Lee Jarvis

foulsham
LONDON • NEW YORK • TORONTO • SYDNEY

foulsham

Bennetts Close, Cippenham, Berkshire SL1 5AP

ISBN 0-572-01772-3

Phototypeset in Great Britain by Typesetting Solutions, Slough, Berks.
Printed and bound in Great Britain by Cox & Wyman Ltd., Reading, Berks.

Contents

Introduction

Why do we *need* to write letters? ... With efficient telephone links between most parts of the world, are letters necessary at all?

There are both advantages and disadvantages to phoning. If all goes well, the great advantage is that of instant reaction and response: 'Mary, I love you, will you marry me?' 'Of course, when?' 'How about next September?' The great disadvantage is perhaps best summed up by: 'Mary, I love you, will you marry me?' ... 'Sorry, this is Joan, shall I get Mary to ring you?' ... or ... 'Sorry, I didn't catch that, could you say it again, please.' ... or ... 'Who is that?' ... or even by a horrified afterthought of the accepted wooer, ' ... What *have* I done? Why on earth didn't I think about this carefully first!'

When we write a letter – even a casual one – we have time to think before we commit ourselves and we provide a permanent copy of exactly what we have said. There will be the wait for a reply, of course, but at least we will feel that the answering letter is similarly thought out, and we can read it time and time again.

Unfortunately, it seems that many of us have forgotten *how* to write letters. Time was, when letter writing was a skill acquired in childhood. Thank-you letters for Christmas and birthday gifts were a 'must'. Often, we struggled desperately, not knowing how to start; but we did learn to communicate by letter. Nowadays, a telephone call or a scribbled name on a 'Thank-you' card is often all that is expected of children, and the skill of letter writing has to be gained in later life. In the early 1990s, servicemen found themselves stationed in a part of the world where telephone communication with home was impossible. It was discovered that, in many cases, they did not know *how* to express themselves in letters to their wives and girlfriends. They could not cope with the kind of communication that did not provide an instant response.

Whether you have forgotten the skill of letter writing, want to brush up your writing technique, or are starting 'from scratch', this book will help. Founded on *The Basildon Bond Letters For Every Occasion*, it will help you to produce exactly the letter you wish to write, with ease. Guidance is given on grammar and spelling, on how to display your letters, on what materials to use, and on how to plan what you write. A wide range of example letters is provided, to cover the sort of common situations in which you may need, or wish, to write a letter. These example letters are listed in the index, for your easy reference.

Dip into the book to find what *you* need to make your letter writing easy and – we trust – enjoyable.

1. Materials and Tools

All that you need is something to write on and something to write with. These are the materials and tools of letter writing.

PAPER AND ENVELOPE

Your writing paper should be of good quality, plain, and unlined. Small sheets, or even notelets, are fine for personal correspondence; sheets of A4 size are preferable for official letters, since they will fit the recipients' files. Whenever possible, the paper and envelope should match.

Types of Paper

Bond is a good quality paper that is crease- and tear-resistant. Usually it is white but pastel shades are available.

Bank is a flimsy paper which is very useful if you wish to make carbon copies of your letters.

Airmail paper is very thin and lightweight and so the cost of overseas postage is kept down.

Types of Envelope

You may have seen references to POP (Post Office Preferred) envelopes and cards. This is a range recommended by the

Post Office to allow the electronic sorting of both business and private mail up to 60 grams in weight. There are various requirements for a card or envelope to be POP. Envelopes should be no smaller than 90 mm by 140 mm and no larger than 120 mm by 235 mm. Envelopes and cards should be oblong with the longer side at least 1.4 times the shorter side, and the cards must be 'rigid'.

TOOLS

The pen or the typewriter is the main tool used in letter writing. If you choose to write by hand, make sure your pen is of reasonable quality so that your words are easy to read and not 'blotchy'. Black or blue ink is preferable. Should you require a copy of your hand-written letter, it is better to get a photocopy made than to press hard when writing in order to get a carbon copy.

If your writing is difficult to read, consider using a typewriter – but do make sure it has a good ribbon. Should you have difficulty in 'thinking' on a typewriter, write your letter by hand, and then copy it in type.

Word Processor

If you have access to a word processor, this can be a great time-saving device, offering the flexibility to make changes, update, correct and duplicate very easily. Sentences or paragraphs can be added or deleted – without you having to start again, as you would with a typed letter. Some word processors will even check and correct your spelling.

When you want several copies of your letter – say, for job applications and CVs or for writing the same message to a number of friends – a word processor can be particularly useful; you'll even be able to change each copy, if you wish, as you go along. Some word processing programmes include a mailing list that you can use as an automatic address book.

2. Presentation of Letters

CONTENT

Before you start to write, think carefully about what you want to say in your letter. Jot down all the points you need to get across, and put them into a reasonable order. You then have a basic structure for the body of your letter with, as far as possible, one main point or idea in each paragraph.

Think about letters you have received. Perhaps you've struggled to work out what is important and what is not in letters that are merely a jumble of thoughts, scribbled down as they occurred to the writer. How would you have welcomed, instead, a letter where the thoughts were in some sort of logical order and separated, each from the next!

If you are writing any sort of business letter, ordering and structuring is of great importance. Generally, the recipient won't give time to working out what you are trying to communicate; *that* must be apparent on a first read-through. And do remember, always be polite and courteous in your business letters; you may feel far from being polite and courteous, but your letters should never reflect this – otherwise they are almost sure to be counter-productive.

PRESENTATION

A badly laid out letter where the writing is straggling or difficult to decipher, or where the typing is ragged, is not likely to create a good impression. It suggests an offhand approach and encourages a similar reaction in the recipient.

A well presented letter, correctly shaped and laid out, with good punctuation, does just the opposite.

LAYOUT

Above the text of the letter there will normally be: the sender's address; the recipient's address; the opening greeting; and, sometimes the sender's and recipient's reference numbers and a heading saying briefly what the letter is about. Below the main text there will be the complimentary close and signature of the sender. The basic layout of these is as follows.

- Sender's address: This goes in the top right corner of the sheet. Each line may be in line with the one above it, or may be indented (the address is 'stepped'), as you choose.

- The date: Leave one line space below the address and then put in the date, starting it in alignment with the first line of the address.

- Recipient's address: This is normally only included in business letters and should match the address on the envelope. Leave a line space under the date and write the address on the left side of the sheet.

- References: These are normally written on separate lines, beginning opposite the first line of the recipient's address and directly below the date.

- The opening greeting: Leave a line space under the recipient's address and begin 'Dear Sir', – or whatever is appropriate – directly below.

- Heading: If used, this should be underlined and placed after the opening greeting, leaving a line space above and below. It may be centred or started at the left side of the sheet, as you choose.

- Main text: Leave a line space between paragraphs, which may be indented or not, as you choose.

- The complimentary close: Leave a line space after the final paragraph. The complimentary close may be written on the left side of the sheet, or towards the right, as you choose.

- The signature: This is hand written directly below the complimentary close. It is helpful if the writer's name is printed (or typed) underneath, and if appropriate, his or her job title or position.

Indented or blocked style?

Example 1 shows a letter correctly laid out in the blocked, or not indented, style. Example 2 shows the same letter laid out in the indented style. Either is correct, but you should not mix the styles.

THE ROMAN WAX TABLET & STYLUS DIDN'T SUIT THE EGYPTIAN SUMMER.

Example 1   Blocked style

Double Dealers
12 Fairview Lane,
Marshgate,
Surrey BX7 2JG

7th October 19__

Mrs J. R. Noakes,   Our ref. PL27B
14 Better Road,
Tinton,   Your ref.
Devon SB9 6PT

Dear Mrs Noakes,

Repairs to new garage doors

I am sorry that you are not satisfied with the
installation of new garage doors that was carried out on
22nd September. However, I cannot agree to carry out the
repairs you ask for without charging a further fee.

It is unfortunate that you accidentally reversed into the
doors, but I am not surprised that the hinges and bolts
broke as a result. I think in this case it would be fair to
blame the car and not poor workmanship on our part.

However, since the repairs needed are fairly minor, I am
prepared to refit the doors and charge only for the cost of
the new hinges and bolts.

I hope this will be satisfactory.

Yours sincerely,

Norman Aldwin
Managing Director

Example 2   Indented style

Double Dealers
12 Fairview Lane,
Marshgate,
   Surrey BX7 2JG

7th October 19__

Mrs J. R. Noakes,   Our ref. PL27B
14 Better Road,
Tinton,   Your ref.
Devon SB9 6PT

Dear Mrs Noakes,

<u>Repairs to new garage doors</u>

   I am sorry that you are not satisfied with the
installation of new garage doors that was carried out on
22nd September. However, I cannot agree to carry out the
repairs you ask for without charging a further fee.

   It is unfortunate that you accidentally reversed
into the doors, but I am not surprised that the hinges and
bolts broke as a result. I think in this case it would be
fair to blame the car and not poor workmanship on our part.

   However, since the repairs needed are fairly minor,
I am prepared to refit the doors and charge only for the
cost of the new hinges and bolts.

   I hope this will be satisfactory.

                              Yours sincerely,

                              Norman Aldwin
                              Managing Director

PUNCTUATION STYLE IN LETTERS

Two methods of punctuation are commonly used in writing letters, excluding the main text where the normal rules of punctuation apply.

The first method, most suitable when writing by hand, is shown in Examples 1 and 2. Each line of the address except the last is followed by a comma, as is the opening greeting and the complimentary close. There is no full stop after the post code, nor after the date, nor after the name or job title of the writer.

Abbreviations such as Rd (Road), Mr (Mister), ref. (reference) and Esq. (Esquire), take a full stop when the last letter of the abbreviation differs from the last letter of the abbreviated word. (In other words only when the word is a true abbreviation and not a contraction.) Thus Esq. and ref. take a full stop, while Rd and Mr do not. The same applies to the initials before a person's name, which take a full stop.

The second method is simply to omit punctuation from all parts of the letter excluding the main text. This is known as the open punctuated style and is most often used together with the blocked style of layout.

HOW TO BEGIN A LETTER

- Dear Sir,   or   Dear Madam,
  Either of these is usual in business correspondence.
- Sir,   or   Madam,
  These are still sometimes used, but are more formal than 'Dear Sir' or 'Dear Madam'.
- Dear Sirs,
  This is the correct opening when a letter is addressed to a company or to 'Messrs So and So'. As an alternative, 'Sirs', can be used if greater formality is required.

- Gentlemen,
  Sometimes used when you wish to be very formal or oratorical.

  Note that a letter begun in any of the above ways does not make it clear to whom it is addressed. It is therefore imperative that, if you are in fact writing to a particular person, his or her name and/or title should appear in the address.

- Dear Mr Jones, or Dear Mrs Brown, or Dear Miss Smith, or Dear Ms Taylor,
  All the above are correct when the writer is personally acquainted with the person receiving the letter or has had previous correspondence with him or her.

- Dear John Brown, or Dear Mary Smith,
  These are now quite acceptable, but are rather less formal than the earlier forms of address.

- Dear Tom, or My Dear Tom,
  These are used between good friends, in either personal or business letters.

- My Darling Tom, or My Dearest Mary,
  These are correct for special cases of affection and should, of course, never be used in a business context.

HOW TO CLOSE A LETTER

- Yours faithfully,
  A safe ending for most business letters when the formal 'Dear Sir' or 'Dear Madam' has been used at the beginning.

- Yours sincerely, or Yours very sincerely,
  Correct for more friendly business letters, written to someone addressed by name, such as 'Dear Mr Smith'.

- Yours sincerely, or Best wishes'
  A safe ending for all personal letters and business letters

where the correspondents are well known to each other.

- Faithfully yours,
  The words can be reversed in this way although the result is slightly pompous.

- Yours respectfully,
  Used in a long letter that is in the form of a report. In other cases, it should be used rarely, since it can seem servile.

- Your obedient servant,
  Used only in certain offical letters.

- Yours affectionately,
  Suitable for relations, would-be relations and between girlfriends.

- Yours ever, or Love,
  Used only when writing to a close friend.

PHRASES FOR BEGINNING LETTERS

If you are looking for a simple phrase with which to start your letter, one of the following could well suit your purpose:

I am very grateful for –
In reply to your letter of –
It was kind of you to –
I am sorry to tell you –
It is so long since you wrote –
I am wondering if you could –
As requested –
Thank you for –
I enclose –
Please –
Thank you for your letter of –
I am sorry to inform you that –
I greatly appreciate your –

With reference to your letter of –
Referring to your letter of –
I am anxious to hear from you concerning –
You may be interested to hear –
We wish to remind you that –
I have to point out –
Your letter gave me –
I have carefully considered your –
I would like to know –
We recently wrote to you about –
Many thanks for the beautiful –
I know that you will be sorry to hear that –
I am delighted to tell you that –
I write to –

ADDRESSING THE ENVELOPE

The address on the envelope gives the recipient a first impression of you. If it is clear and well laid out, the impression will be favourable; if it is unclear and messy, it may never arrive, let alone impress the receiver!

Start addressing your envelopes about halfway down and towards the middle. The addressee's name goes in the first line, and then the actual address follows, in lines, exactly as in the letter. You may use the blocked or indented style, to match that used in the letter.

The Post Office makes the following requests to addressers of envelopes.

- Use the house number, if it has one, not just the house name. Similarly, give the number allocated to flats, offices, etc.

- Write the name of the street, road, etc., but only add the district within a town if there is more than one street of that name in the town. In country districts, however, the name of the hamlet or village should be given.

- Write the postal town (the centre to which the mail is sent) and then the county of that town. For large postal towns or cities – such as London or Bristol – and those that give their name to counties – such as Gloucester – the county is not written.

- Write the postal code, clearly, at the end of the last line or as a separate line at the end of the address.

Here are some examples. The open punctuation style has been used, but make sure that the style you choose matches that of your letter.

Mr B.A. Williams	John Davidson Esq.
Willows	Flat 2
34 High Road	38 Victoria Road
BROUGHTON	WESTBURY
Sussex BR5 4TR	Surrey W17 9UG

Note: Esq. and Mr are alternative forms for addressing men; they must not be used together. Esq. (with a full stop) is the abbreviation for Esquire, and is generally used with letters beginning 'Dear Sir'. Never use 'Davidson Esq.'. If the first name or initials are not known, write 'Mr Davidson'.

Ms P. Turnbull	Mrs Jane Philips
51 Cadogan Avenue	54 Wharf Rd
WELLFORD	West Bridgford
Lancs LA8 2FE	Hampshire GU9 4TR

Notes: Ms may be used if you do not know if the addressee is married or single, or if she prefers to be addressed as Ms. At one time, Mrs Jane Philips would have been correctly addressed as 'Mrs Paul Philips' or 'Mrs P. Philips' – by her husband's given name or initials, if her husband was still alive. Nowadays, many women prefer to be addressed by their own given name. A further point of interest: this (invented) West Bridgford is, geographically, located in Hampshire, but has a Guildford (Surrey) post code. Counties such as Hampshire – Hants – and Lancashire – Lancs – that can be abbreviated, may be written in either form.

3. Grammar and Punctuation

The gap between what we get away with in speech and what is correct in writing is a major problem to many would-be letter writers. The rules of English grammar may seem very complicated, but they have been established to ensure that the written message communicates with the reader and does not confuse or cause misunderstanding.

Fortunately, the average letter writer doesn't need to be an expert in the rules of grammar. All that is needed is a familiarity with the structure of correct sentences and proper punctuation. If you know how to write and punctuate a sentence correctly and if you avoid writing long and complicated sentences, your readers will receive the message you intend, clearly.

In this chapter we look at sentences and punctuation and briefly at spelling. There is also a section on common pitfalls that you should note and so avoid in your letters.

THE SENTENCE

The sentence is a group of words that make complete sense. To make complete sense it must contain a subject (a word or words about which the sentence says something) and a predicate (a word or words about the subject). As a simple example: 'The boy ate an apple.' is a sentence. 'The boy' is the subject and 'ate an apple' is the predicate.

Guidelines

• You should avoid splitting the subject and the predicate.

  Do not write:
    David, after hitting John in the playground, apologised.
  Write, instead:
    After hitting John in the playground, David apologised.

• You should avoid splitting infinitives (to run, to speak etc.)

  Do not write:
    Peter wanted to carefully and meticulously clean the family car.
  Write, instead:
    Peter wanted to clean the family car carefully and meticulously.

• You should not change the subject within a sentence.

  Do not write:
    We were cold on the beach because one felt the wind.
  Write, instead:
    We were cold on the beach because we felt the wind.

• You should not change the tense in your sentence.

  Do not write:
    Jane answered the telephone but nobody speaks.
  Write, instead:
    Jane answered the telephone but nobody spoke.

SOME GRAMMATICAL PITFALLS

Collective nouns
Collective nouns are nouns which are singular in form but

refer to a group of persons or things. You must be careful to use a singular or plural verb depending on the purpose of the particular sentence.

The committee was furious with the plans for a strike.
That is, the committee was acting as a group.

The committee were arguing among themselves over the plans for a strike.
That is, the committee were obviously acting as individuals, not as a unit.

Pronouns and adjectives
The most common error involving pronouns is in phrases using 'me' and 'I'. For example, 'between you and I' is wrong and should be 'between you and me'.

Another error is in the use of 'myself'.
It is correct to write:
'I washed myself' and 'I don't believe that, myself'.
It is not correct to write:
My wife and myself watched the film.
Write, instead:
My wife and I saw the film.

Similar to the problem of the collective noun is the problem of 'distributive' adjectives and pronouns. These are: anybody, nobody, everybody, either, neither, each, every, none. They are all singular, and must be used with verbs or pronouns in the singular.
Do not write:
Everybody who travels abroad must have their passports.
Write, instead:
Everybody who travels abroad must have his or her passport.
And, do not write:
Each of the children were given balloons after the party.
Write, instead:
Each of the children was given a balloon after the party.

Verbs

Verbs are singular or plural depending on the singular or plural nature of their subject.

It is correct to write, either:

Those dishes, left from Julie's party, have not been washed.

Or, to write:

That stack of dishes, left from Julie's party, has not been washed.

The use of 'and', is like the plus sign in mathematics and makes a plural total. For example:

John and Kathy were at the restaurant.

If we use any other words to join John and Kathy, this does not happen.

John, as well as his girlfriend Kathy, was at the restaurant.

Adverbs

The most common mistake here is to use an adjective when an adverb is required.

Do not write:

She ate the biscuits very quick.

Write, instead:

She ate the biscuits very quickly.

Prepositions

Avoid using the prepositional phrase 'due to' when 'because of' conveys the correct idea.

Do not write:

The cricket match was stopped due to the rain.

Write, instead:

The cricket match was stopped because of the rain.

Avoid using the verb 'following' when prepositions and pre-positional phrases such as 'after', 'because of', 'as a result of', and 'in accordance with', are more accurate.

Do not write:

Following the heavy rains, the roads flooded.

Write, instead:

Because of the heavy rains, the roads flooded.

or:

After the heavy rains, the roads flooded.

Miscellaneous errors

The use of 'than'.

Do not write:

John is cleverer than me.

This is incorrect because the complete sentence would be:

John is cleverer than I am.

Write, instead:

John is cleverer than I.

The use of 'less' and 'fewer'.

'Fewer' should be used when the persons or object can be counted. Use 'less' when what is referred is a quantity or an amount.

Write:

James ate no fewer than four biscuits at tea.

James takes less sugar in his tea than I do.

PUNCTUATION

The most commonly used punctuation marks in English are:

full stop	.
colon	:
semicolon	;
comma	,
parentheses	( )
question mark	?
exclamation mark	!
quotation marks	' '
apostrophe	'

Full stop
Every declarative sentence must end with a full stop.

Colon
The colon signals that an explanation or more information follows.

It is used to introduce a series.
 The child wanted three things for Christmas: a large stuffed animal, some coloured paper, and a small bicycle.

It is used to introduce a quotation, usually a rather lengthy one.
 My mother's favourite saying is from Mark Twain: 'Work consists of whatever a body is obliged to do . . . Play consists of whatever a body is not obliged to do.'

It is used to separate two clauses of equal weight.
 Paul said it was time for supper: I said we had just finished lunch.

Semicolon
This functions mainly in a long sentence to separate clauses where a pause greater than a comma and less than a full stop is needed.

Comma
The comma is the most frequently used punctuation mark.

It is used to separate items in a list of three or more words.

It is used to separate phrases which depend on the same word.
 I have travelled in Canada in a canoe, in Egypt on a camel, and in England on a train.

It is used in a long sentence when a natural pause occurs.

Parentheses (sometimes known as brackets)
These are used in pairs when the writer has an interruption or

aside not necessarily relevant to the main idea of the sentence. Sometimes dashes are used instead of parentheses.

Question mark
This is used at the end of a sentence that is a direct question.

Is there any milk on the doorstep?

Do not use for an indirect question.

Mother asked if there was any milk on the doorstep.

Exclamation mark
This is used at the end of a sentence when a strong feeling is present. A single exclamation mark is enough.

Quotation marks
These are used in pairs to enclose direct quotations.

He asked, 'Where is my umbrella?'

Apostrophe
The apostrophe is used to indicate an omission as in won't, can't or it's. You should note a common pitfall here. It's means it is; the apostrophe must never be used with its in the possessive form (meaning belonging to it).

The apostrophe is, however, used to show possession in other cases.

This is Mary's hat (singular)
Where are the boy's clothes? (singular boy)
Where are the boys' clothes? (plural; more than one boy)

But, as stated above:

Here is its cover.

CAPITAL LETTERS

You should use an initial capital letter:

• to begin a new sentence

- to begin a full quotation
- to indicate proper nouns or adjectives (England, Englishman)
- for the names and titles of people and the names of companies, books, films, newspapers, etc.
- to name specific courses (A level)
- for the days of the week and the months.

You should not use a capital letter for the seasons of the year or for general classes (for example: He wants to be president, but, he is President Clinton).

SPELLING

It is worthwhile to keep a dictionary close by when you write your letters. Even simple words that you use in conversation every day can be a problem when you come to write them down. Take, for example, your sister's daughter: is she your 'neice' or your 'niece'?

A simple jingle to help you with 'ie' and 'ei' words is as follows.

I before E, when sounded as E, except after C,
Or when sounded as A, as in neighbour and weigh.

There are so many rules and exceptions to rules in spelling that the most useful advice that can be offered here is: if you are in any doubt at all, check your dictionary – and then try to remember the correct spelling for the next time you need to write the word.

Example Letters

NOTE: In the Example Letters, generally the address of the sender and the date have not been included, to save space.

4. Invitations and Replies

The most important thing to remember when you are drafting an invitation, either written or printed, is to give details of the time, type of event and your own name.

The style of your invitation is quite important; a formal invitation suggests a formal event, and so on. If you wish to make a formal invitation more personal for close friends, you can write a few friendly words in one corner.

It is usual to reply to an invitation – to say whether or not you are able to attend – in the same style as the invitation. Your reply can be handwritten or typed.

This chapter provides you with some examples and replies that you can adapt to your own requirements.

1 Wedding invitation (formal)

Mr and Mrs John Fowler

request the pleasure of
the company of

(write the name of the guest(s))
at the marriage of their daughter
Marjorie
to
Mr Robert Blake

(cont.)

at Saint Fellows Church
Ringway
on Saturday 29th May
at 2.45 pm
and afterwards at a reception at
The Bullbrook Inn, Ringway

RSVP
21 Drum Lane
Ringway
Somerset PS9 4TJ

OR

Mr and Mrs John Fowler
request the pleasure of your company
at the marriage of their daughter
Marjorie
to
Mr Robert Blake
etc.

If the number of guests is quite low, the invitations may be written by hand on suitable attractive stationery. Usually, however, they are printed. The traditional colour for the lettering is black. Write in the name of the guest or guests by hand. In the example above the correct position is in the top left corner of the card.

RSVP means 'please reply', from the French 'répondez s'il vous plaît'.

OR

The exact wording depends on who is issuing the invitation and their relationship to the bride. For example, if the bride's parents are divorced and her mother has remarried, the wording could be:

Mr and Mrs William Stevens
request the pleasure of
the company of

(write in the name of the guest(s))
at the marriage of her
daughter
June Smith
etc.

Although the bride's surname is rarely included in the word-ing, it can be appropriate where it differs from that of the host and hostess.

---

2 Reply to an invitation to a wedding (formal)

(address)

Mr and Mrs Peter Faulkener thank Mr and Mrs John Fowler for their kind invitation to their daughter's wedding, and to the reception, and will be most happy to attend.

OR

... and much regret that a prior engagement prevents them from attending.

It is not necessary to give your full address when the reply is in the form of a brief note, so long as you establish your identity.

---

3 Wedding invitation (informal)

Rachel and Michael Basset
Sylvia and Andrew hope you'll join them, to
celebrate their wedding at Saint Paul's Church,
Littlerow, on Thursday 12th August at 1.30 pm and   (cont.)

at a reception afterwards at the Two Drakes Restaurant, Littlerow.

RSVP
14 Cedars Close
Littlerow
Surrey MT4 1DL

An informal invitation is most often used in the case of a second marriage or for a small wedding party of close friends.

---

4 Reply to an invitation to a wedding (informal)

Sylvia and Andrew

Thank you very much for inviting us to the wedding and reception on 12th August. Of course we will be delighted to attend.

Rachel and Michael Basset
The Tudors
Littlerow

---

5 Announcing an engagement (informal)

(address and date)

Dear Auntie

I simply had to write to tell you the most marvellous news. Robert and I are engaged!

The wedding will be quite soon and of course we will be sending you an invitation when we have the time and the place sorted out.

I do hope you'll be able to come.

Love

Marjorie   (sign)

---

6   Engagement party invitations (informal)

Rachel and Michael Basset

Sylvia and Andrew have great pleasure in inviting you to their engagement party (OR hope you'll join them at their engagement party) at the Green Lees Hotel, Littlerow, on Saturday 24th July at 8.30 pm.

RSVP
14 Cedars Close
Littlerow
Surrey MT4 1DL

This invitation may be written by hand and set out as shown, or printed, with the layout in a central position as for a formal invitation.

7   Reply to an invitation to an engagement party (informal)

Sylvia and Andrew

Thank you very much for inviting us to your engagement party on 24th July. Of course we shall be delighted to attend.

Rachel and Michael Basset
The Tudors
Littlerow

8   Engagement party invitation (formal)

(address)

Mr and Mrs John Fowler
request the pleasure of
the company of

(write in the name of the guest(s))
at an evening party
on Saturday 14th March
at 8.30 pm
at the above address to
celebrate the engagement of their daughter
Marjorie
to
Mr Robert Blake

RSVP

An invitation such as this would usually be printed. If the party is to be at a hotel or other premises, give that address in the main part of the invitation, and the home address at the bottom left, under RSVP.

9   Reply to an invitation to an engagement party (formal)

(address)

Mr and Mrs Peter Faulkener have great pleasure in accepting Mr and Mrs John Fowler's invitation for Saturday, 14th March.

OR

Mr and Mrs Peter Faulkener wish to thank Mr and Mrs John Foster
for their kind invitation for (to their daughters engagement party on)
Saturday 14th March and very much regret that they will be unable
to attend.

---

10   Christening invitation

(address and date)

Dear Mary

John Andrew is due to be christened at St Michael's Church on Sunday 31st April and Mark and I would love you to be there.

The christening is at 3.30 pm, and there is a little celebration at
home afterwards.

If you could arrive here between 2.30 and 3.00 pm, that would
be perfect.

I do hope you will be able to come.

Love

Lindsay   (sign)

---

11   Reply to an invitation to a christening

(address and date)

Dear Lindsay

Thank you so much for inviting me to John Andrew's christening on
Sunday, I wouldn't miss it for the world.

I should arrive by 3.00 pm, but if I am delayed, don't wait, I'll go
straight to St Michael's.

(cont.)

Looking forward to seeing you and Mark again, and of course, the baby.

Love

Mary   (sign)

OR

Dear Lindsay

I do hope you will forgive me when I tell you that I will not be able to make the christening on Sunday.

I am going on holiday in two days' time to Malta, and cannot change the booking now.

It was very kind of you to ask me. You know I would have loved to have been there.

Expect a postcard from Malta. I'll be thinking of you.

Love to John Andrew.

Mary   (sign)

---

12   Children's party invitation

(address and date)

Dear Mrs Alston

Elizabeth and David are having a few of their friends to a party here, on Tuesday 3rd January, and hope that John will be able to come. The party is between 4.30 and 9.00 pm.

If you are thinking of coming to fetch him, it would be nice if you arrived at about 7.00 pm, in time for some of the fun!

(cont.)

Do try to manage this, as I would be very pleased to see you.

Yours sincerely

Judith Trury   (sign)

This letter is, of course, written by the mother of Elizabeth and David. If both mothers are friends, naturally only first names are used. Writing individual letters is not always possible for a busy mum or dad. You will find that you can easily buy pre-printed invitation letters, complete with tear-off reply slips.

---

13 Reply to an invitation to a children's party

(address and date)

Dear Mrs Trury

John says 'thank you very much' for the invitation to the party on 3rd January. He is excited about it and hopes to come.

I will drop in at about 7.00 pm as you suggest, to lend a willing hand.

Looking forward to seeing you.

Yours sincerely

Lyn Alston   (sign)

OR

John is most upset that he will be unable to accept the invitation for the party on 3rd January.

We are going away to stay with my parents over Christmas and will be away for two weeks.

Will you please thank Elizabeth and David and tell them how sorry John is that he will not be able to come?

It was so nice of you to ask him.

Yours sincerely

Lyn Alston   (sign)

---

14   Letter of thanks after a party (childrens)

(address and date)

Dear Mrs Ulston

I thought I'd just write to say thank you very much for inviting David to the party last week.

He hasn't stopped talking about all the games he played and all the presents he won! It sounds as if all the children had a wonderful time.

Thank you again for having David. I hope he wasn't too much of a handful!

Yours sincerely

Margaret Birdham   (sign)

15   Letter of thanks for a present (child)

(address and date)

Dear Uncle George

Thank you very much for sending me the Sherlock Holmes book for my birthday.

Mummy and Daddy bought me a watch and I got lots of other presents but yours is the nicest. I'm really enjoying reading it.

Love

James   (sign)

5. Love, Courtship, Marriage and Family

Love letters are the most highly personal of all forms of correspondence and it would be misleading to try and lay down rules for this sort of writing. The best thing is to simply *be yourself*. Do not aim for a highly literary style or your letters will look artificial. Try to write as you would talk to your loved one. Here, it is not the layout or the grammatical excellence that counts, but the sincerity of your feeling.

The normal rules for beginning and ending letters do not apply for love letters. Although *Dearest James, Darling Sandra,* or simply *Darling* are often used, originality – when it's not merely being clever – is half the charm of a love letter. Similarly with the ending. You can hardly leave out the word love altogether, but the exact wording is entirely up to you.

It is, however, best not to overdo endearments such as kisses or hearts, or they will lose their value. Do not put X's or cryptic messages on the backs of envelopes. Whoever receives the letter will probably not thank you for letting everyone, including the postman, know about the relationship.

The letters that follow can only show one style of writing a love, or family, letter. If they sound 'wrong' to you, don't use them. At best, they are merely a framework for your own personal sentiments. You may, or may not, wish to give your address at the top of your letter. It is probably a good idea to write in the date.

16   Love Letter from a man

(date)

Dearest Lisa

Another Monday – and there's still a long week to go before I'll see you again. It will seem more like a year to me!

I'm writing this in the canteen over a cup of coffee, but somehow it doesn't feel as if I'm really back at work at all. I'm still thinking about all the wonderful things we said and did during our lovely weekend.

I'll have to work late on Thursday and Friday. Maybe it will make the time go faster, although I think even if I could see you every moment of every day it wouldn't be enough!

I'll have to go now darling, back to the grindstone. I'm getting looks from Dunnerton. He'll be over in a minute to see what I'm doing.

Write very soon – and remember, I love you.

Martin

17   Reply to a love letter from a man

(date)

Dearest Martin

Your letter came at last, this morning. I saw the postman halfway down the road and decided to hang on, just hoping.

I read it three times on the way into work. I think I know it by heart now. I'll never forget our wonderful weekend, will you?

(cont.)

I long for us to be together again and I'm wishing away the days until our holiday! Last night I dreamed we were walking hand in hand along a deserted beach and then swimming in the sea, and then ... !

Love is ... well, we know what it is, don't we? I guess it's also hanging on for the postman when you're late for work already!

All my love, always

Lisa

---

18   Love letter from a serviceman who is posted overseas

(date)

Ann Darling

It seems forever since I was with you, instead of three long months. If only I could phone. I long for the sound of your voice. Do you miss me as much as I miss you?

I won't say I wish you were here with me, because it's not such a good place to be. Still, we all hope and pray things will soon get sorted out and we can – as they say in the films – 'get the hell out of here'.

It was great to get your letter telling me all about your Christmas. Thanks for calling in on Mum and Dad; I heard from Mum the other day and she said how happy they were to see you and – as she always does – asked when we were going to get married and give her some grandchildren!

All things considered, we had a good Christmas out here. Plenty to eat and drink and our parcels from home turned up in good time. A thousand thanks for the sweater. It fits perfectly and is quite beautiful. You must have been knitting away every evening since we parted.

(cont.)

Well, my love, another letter comes to an end. You know all the things I want to say to you, don't you? Perhaps it won't be too long now. Write back soon, won't you – I need your letters so much.

All my love, now and always

Terry

---

19 Love letter to a serviceman who is posted overseas

(date)

Dearest Terry

It was so good to hear from you. Yes, love, I miss you too – more than you could imagine.

All of us at home send our love and we hope that you and the lads can keep cheerful. We saw a TV report about the area you are in and saw all the snow. I'm glad you liked the sweater and it fitted; I reckon you'll need it when you are off duty.

We had our first snow of the winter last week and Jane and I took her kids on to the hill for a spot of tobogganing. It was great fun, but walking on the hill brought back so many memories of us together there, last summer, that I got a bit weepy. Fingers crossed that we can go there again, together, before too long.

Jenny and all the other girls at the supermarket send their love to you. I shouldn't tell you this, but I heard they are planning to send you a stack of Valentine cards. Perhaps you'll be able to pass one or two of them to Sam and Pete, anonymously of course. I feel so sad that they have no one to write to or to hear from; it might cheer them up a bit.

(cont.)

I have to close now so I can catch the post. I miss you so much, and you know how much I love you. Take good care of yourself and come home to me soon. I'll write again at the weekend, when I hope I'll have had another letter from you.

My love, for ever and ever

Ann

---

20 Family letter from a serviceman overseas

(date)

Dear Peggy, Joanne and Wayne

Only six more months and four more days and we'll all be together again. Like you, I'm crossing off the days from the calendar.

Thanks for your last letter, Peg; I was thrilled to read that Wayne has said his first word. Are you sure it was Dad he said? I hope you are managing all right, love. I wish your Mum was nearer to help you out. Still, Joanne is a great kid, isn't she; and it's good you were able to get her into playschool.

We're having mixed weather and it's quite stormy at present. We are kept hard at it, so we don't have too much time to get homesick, thank goodness. The lads are a good crowd and we try to keep the youngsters from getting too fed up. Mind you, I don't know how we'd all cope if football hadn't been invented.

There are rumours that we might get our phone line fixed this month. There will be a long queue to phone home if they get it working again, but I'll be right at the front just to have a few words and to know, for sure, that you are all well.

Write soon and let me know all the news, won't you. Give the kids a big hug from their Dad.

My love to you all

Steve

---

21 Reply from family to a serviceman overseas

(date)

Dear Steve

I had to read your last letter to Joanne four or five times. She really does miss you, and so, of course, do I.

We are all well apart from summer colds. Having a bit of time while Joanne is at playschool is a great help and I've started to decorate the bedroom. I'm enclosing a piece of the wallpaper and hope that you like what I've chosen.

Wayne can say long sentences now, and they all seem to start with 'Dad'. We haven't worked out the other words yet; Joanne says she thinks her brother is speaking in Japanese!

When Betty came round last month she took these two snaps of us in the garden. As you'll see, young Tom has a small bicycle and, of course, Joanne has been on and on at me ever since to get her one for her birthday. What do you think? I could probably find a good secondhand one and I'd make her promise she wouldn't take it out of the garden.

We all hope it won't be too long before you can phone home. Just to be able to talk together would be great, wouldn't it? Still, as Mum always says, I shouldn't have married a soldier if I couldn't cope when you went overseas.

Don't worry about us; we're all fine and we all send you all our love. Be good! Miss you and love you.

Peggy, Joanne and Wayne

PROPOSALS OF MARRIAGE

Proposals of marriage are almost always made verbally. The reasons are obvious. Even a stammered proposal is more likely to be favourably received than a beautifully written letter. If you write because you fear rejection you will probably have your fear confirmed!

A proposal should be made by letter only when there are special circumstances that make a verbal proposal impracticable – usually when there is a long distance between the two parties. If it is impossible to overcome this – as it may be, for example, in the case of military service or overseas employment – then a letter is justified.

Courtship by correspondence is best done gradually; a proposal should be led up to in previous letters. The form of the proposal will depend a great deal on what has been said before, but the important thing is that there should be no noticeable change of style. The following letter should be read with that in mind.

---

22 Proposing marriage, from a man

(address and date)

Darling

You must know how much I miss you and want to be with you. I've told you so many times in my letters – and my love for you just gets stronger with each day that we're apart.

Perhaps if I were home I could say what I'm going to write, but I can't put it off any longer. So here it is: darling, will you marry me?

I know I can't offer you much, and I don't even know how long I'll be stuck out here in the wilds. But it can't be for much longer, and the waiting will be less unbearable if I can think that the end will be the beginning of a new life with you.

(cont.)

Darling, if this sounds clumsy and contrived, it's because it isn't easy to express feelings like this in a letter. I only hope you can read between the lines and guess just how much I really love and want you.

You have . . . all my love

Don

---

23   Postponing an answer to a proposal of marriage

(address and date)

Dearest Don

I was very flattered to receive your proposal – although I must admit, it has rather taken me by surprise.

Don, you know that I care for you very much. I really do. But, just now, I honestly don't know whether I love you enough to marry you. I didn't know you for very long when you were in England, and I won't really know how I feel until I see you again.

I know it's unsatisfactory not to answer clearly 'yes' or 'no', but marriage is such a big step that I think we just need more time together before making a decision.

Perhaps you will find that I'm not quite all you've imagined while you're away. I should hate you to come back and find that you feel differently.

Don, if you are willing to wait to see how it works out, I am too. I still haven't met anyone half as nice as you. If I didn't truly believe that it was the best way for both of us, I would never take this risk of losing you altogether.

Please phone me as soon as you are able.

Love

Erica

---

24 Accepting a proposal of marriage

(address and date)

Dear darling Don

Yes – but yes, of course I will marry you.

But that is just to confirm my telemessage. I do hope your office got the message to you. This air mail is too slow for me! I can't wait for you to get to a phone again, so we can talk together.

I have told Mother and Father and of course they are tremendously pleased. You know they always did approve of you.

I can hardly wait until you're home. The weeks seem to pass so slowly; it's quite unbearable. Perhaps I should turn my mind to 'marriage plans' – the bridesmaids, the wedding, the honeymoon, somewhere to live! You see, I'm getting quite carried away!

Seriously Don, I miss you like crazy! Write soon. I'm dreaming of you all the time. And I'm so very happy.

All my love

Erica

25 Not accepting a proposal of marriage

(address and date)

Dearest Don

You have paid me the greatest compliment any woman can receive and the least I can do is to give you my answer promptly and frankly. Don, I care very much about you – but I'm afraid the answer is no.

(cont.)

It would be easy for me to say that we didn't know each other well enough, or that I'm not sure about my feelings towards you. But that would be untrue.

Please don't take it too much to heart when I tell you that although I like and admire you tremendously, I'm not in love with you – and I know that I never shall be.

Don, I'm not worth your regrets. I've risked hurting your feelings because I don't want you to go on wasting your hopes on me. I hope you will understand, and will always think of me as,

Your very good friend

Erica

---

26 Breaking off an engagement/relationship

(date)

Dear Ian

Your letter arrived this morning. It was so nice that it makes what I've got to say sound awful. It's not meant to be.

Ian, I think that for some time we've both been pretending to each other. Maybe we were in love at first and if so, I don't know how or why it changed, but I know now that although I'm very fond of you, I can never really love you truly.

It's painful to me to write this and it's taken a long time to put pen to paper. But I'm sure you will agree it's best to be honest.

We're bound to see each other again and I hope that when we do, we can still be very good friends.

Yours sincerely

Laura

This letter could equally well be written by a man to a woman.

---

27 Felicitations to a mother on her daughter's engagement

(address and date)

Dear Celia

May I as an old friend send my felicitations on Mary's engagement to David which I saw announced in the paper yesterday.

You must be very pleased. David and Mary seem such a suited young couple that I'm sure you need have no fears for their future happiness.

Do give my love and very best wishes to Mary.

Yours sincerely

Margaret Roberts

28 Thanks for a wedding present

(address and date)

Dear Auntie Mabel

How kind of you and Uncle James to send us such a beautiful coffee service as a wedding present. You may be sure it will see plenty of use once David and I are settled in our new home. Thank you from both of us.

We are looking forward to having you with us at the wedding. I hope you will both come to see us after the honeymoon – and find out just how good the coffee really is!

Yours affectionately

Mary

29 Congratulations on a silver wedding anniversary

(address and date)

Dear Tom

It's just 25 years since I proposed a toast to a smiling groom and his lovely bride and wished them a long and happy life together.

My wishes were well founded. You and Geraldine have every right to feel pleased with yourselves. I know of only one other couple who have been as happy together as you – and you can probably guess who I mean!

Ann joins me in wishing you many more years of happiness together. We enclose a little memento of the occasion – and I hope that we shall be able to send you another one, in gold, in 25 years' time.

Yours sincerely

Chris

30 Acknowledgement of a letter of congratulation on a silver wedding anniversary

(address and date)

Dear Chris

It was very kind of you to think of us on our silver wedding anniversary.

Geraldine and I were absolutely delighted with your letter and the lovely Wedgwood vase which is now filled with flowers and has pride of place on the dining room table.

It really was a very nice gesture indeed, and one which Geraldine and I look forward to reciprocating next year when you join us in this silvered respectability.

Our thanks and best wishes to you and Ann.

Yours sincerely

Tom

6. Appointments

When writing to a prospective employer, it is important to remember that the letter will be your ambassador. It will create an impression of you in the mind of the recipient on the basis of which he will decide whether or not to short-list you. Obviously you must write, or type, your letter neatly, laying it out according to the conventions described in Chapter Two. You should include all the *relevant* information, but avoid unnecessary details; remember that the person to whom you are writing is probably very busy and will, no doubt, receive dozens of applications for the job. Do not be afraid to let your character show through your letter, but try not to become chatty.

If you are applying for a post which may involve typing, the letter should be typed as a perfect example of your skill. In other cases, a neatly written letter will create a better impression than a badly-typed one, but a well-typed letter would be better still.

In all cases, decide what you want to say before you start writing; write as simply and clearly as possible, and avoid clichés and pompous language which you would not use in ordinary speech.

CURRICULUM VITAE IN GENERAL

The object of a curriculum vitae (sometimes abbreviated to CV) is to set out the bare details of your education, employment and personal status as a reference or quick guide for the person who requested it. You should always include your name, address and date of birth, and it is normal to give the names and addresses of two referees (i.e. persons the recipient can refer to regarding your status).

Your CV is not the place to write a descriptive essay; just state the facts. It should be written on a separate sheet of paper, enclosed with an explanatory letter, and should be as clearly laid out as possible.

31 Curriculum vitae (1)

Name: Jane Brown

Address: 43 Chalcot Park
          London NW1 6AX

Telephone: home 071 485 0396
            office 071 822 3065

Date of birth: October 7th 1970

Marital status: single

Secondary education: St Mark's School
                      Edgware
                      Middlesex TP4 3SZ
                      1981-1987
                      5 GCSEs   English Language   (C)
                                     Mathematics   (C)
                                     Geography   (D)
                                     Art   (E)
                                     English Literature   (E)

Employment: Clerical Assistant with Jones Bros Ltd, Tower Road, London N1 2ER, 1988 – date.

Referees: Mr S Colins
              Jones Bros Ltd
              Tower Road
              London N1 2ER

              Mrs R Smith
              Headmistress
              St Mark's School
              Edgware
              Middlesex TP4 3SZ

32 Curriculum vitae (2)

Name: John Smith

Address: 69 Lower Terrace
            Onsworth
            Bedfordshire DF7 2SJ

Telephone: home Onsworth 638006
                office Onsworth 534662

Date of birth: 8th August 1948

Marital status: married

Education since 11   Penworthy Grammar School
                                          Penworthy
                                          Bedfordshire FT2 6PN
                                          1959 – 66
                                          6 'O' levels
                                          3 'A' levels   History Grade B
                                                              Geography Grade C
                                                              Latin Grade C

                                          Manchter University
                                          1966 – 69

                                          BA (History) Second Class Hons.

Employment: Management Trainee with Unitech Limited, Unitech
                   House, Queen St, Onsworth DB6 6TZ, 1970 – 71;
                   promoted to Assistant Manager (sales) 1971 – 75;
                   Area Manager (marketing) with Framley (UK) Ltd,
                   Hope House, Thorpe Way, Onsworth DJ2 2PT,
                   1975 – date.

Referees: Mr K Park
                     Faculty of Arts
                     Manchter University
                     Manchter FP6 2NP

                     Mr B Crane
                     Managing Director
                     Framley (UK) Ltd
                     Hope House
                     Thorpe Way
                     Onsworth DJ2 2PT

When you apply for an advertised position but are already in employment, explain why you wish to change your job, otherwise it might be assumed that you are leaving at your employer's behest.

33 Application for a position as a secretary/typist

(address and date)

Crumb & Cake Limited
154-158 Church Way
Cartown
Yorks SL8 5RC

Dear Sirs

I write in answer to your advertisement in this week's *Cartown Chronicle* for a secretary/typist with word processing experience.

I am twenty-one years old, and was educated at Mallow Comprehensive where I obtained good GCSE passes in English Language, French, Mathematics, Secretarial Studies and Home Economics.

For the past two years I have been working in the Personnel Department of J. Jones and Sons, as a junior shorthand-typist. My speeds are 100 wpm for shorthand and 60 wpm for typing.

Although I enjoy my present job, I am keen to find a post with more responsibility where I can use my word processing skills.

My Departmental Manager, Mr Brian Lovell, has agreed to give me time off to come for an interview on any afternoon other than Thursdays, and is also willing to write a reference.

Yours faithfully

Susan Brown   (sign)

34 Application for a position as a clerical officer

(address and date)

Mr J. Braid
Sales Director
Messrs F R Sims and Sons Limited
Friary Road
Northley WJ4 1SX

Dear Sir

I write in answer to your advertisement for a Senior Clerical
Officer in last Friday's *Evening Post.*

I am thirty years of age, unmarried and in good health. I was
educated at St Anne's Convent, Northley, where I obtained four
GCE 'O' levels in English Language, History, Geography and
Mathematics. I then went to Northey Polytechnic where I took a
course in office procedures and business methods.

After various temporary posts, I secured a position as Junior
Clerical Officer at Smith & Jones Limited, York Way, Northey,
where I stayed for ten years. During that time I was promoted to
Senior Ledger Clerk, a post I held until the firm was closed last
year. I am now doing temporary work again, but am very
anxious to find secure employment, and I hope you will look
favourably on my application.

I would be able to come for an interview at any time, but would
much appreciate three days' notice for the convenience of the
agency whose books I am currently on. I can provide excellent
references should you so wish.

Yours faithfully

Caroline Brown   (sign)

35   Application for a position as a computer programmer

(address and date)

Personnel Officer
Perry Computers Limited
18-22 Milton Close
Milton Trading Estate
London N19 6XJ

Dear Sir

I would like to apply for the position of Computer Programmer which was advertised in the 9th March issue of *Computer Weekly*.

I enclose my curriculum vitae, from which you will see that I was born and educated in London and have seven years experience as a computer programmer.

During my five years with Brown and Company I have gained experience of a wide variety of programmes and techniques, including the new beta software system. I would now like to further my career by specialising in the fields which your advertisement mentions.

I would be happy to come for an interview at any time.

Yours faithfully

Harry Singh   (sign)

Enc.

There is no need to go into detail about your work experience and qualifications providing your CV covers these adequately.

36 Reply to an invitation to attend an interview

(address and date)

J George Esq.
Kingley Marketing
64 King Street
Milton
Northants SY7 8PL

Dear Mr George

Thank you very much for your letter of 13th May. I would be happy to come for an interview on 21st May at 2.00 pm, and will bring with me the references you request.

Yours sincerely

Brian Butts   (sign)

It is important to send a letter in this situation, not merely as confirmation that you will attend, but also to show that you are taking the matter seriously and paying attention to detail.

37 Accepting an offer of employment

(address and date)

R Burns Esq.
Personnel Manager
Timetec Limited
Rose Estate
Oxridge
Bucks SL9 5RF

Dear Mr Burns

Thank you for your letter of 12th October offering me the post of Ledger Clerk with your organisation.

I am delighted to accept the position and look forward to starting work with you on 15th November.

Yours sincerely

Jane Allcock   (sign)

38   Resignation letter

(address and date)

M Broad Esq.
Personnel Manager
Flight and Pearce Limited
Malford
Berks YO9 3PM

Dear Mr Broad

I have to inform you that I have been offered the position of
Chief Buyer with Smith and Allsopp of 19 High Street, and I
have accepted the post since it will give me greater responsibility
and an increased salary. I wish, therefore, to tender my
resignation as from 31st July.

I would like to take this opportunity to say how much I have
enjoyed working at Flight and Pearce. Nevertheless I feel that I
owe it to myself and my family to further my career by making
this move, and would like to thank you for giving me the
training and experience which have made such a promotion
possible.

Yours sincerely

Simon Jones   (sign)

7. Domestic Matters

Letters in this chapter cover a wide variety of topics – schools, repairs to household items, goods bought, complaints, house purchases, etc. Because of the diversity of the subject matter, perhaps the best advice for you, the letter writer, is to remember to reach the point of your letter quickly, giving all the facts that you feel are relevant to the subject of the letter. Do remember to include your address, the date, and any reference numbers. In some cases you may like to also include your phone number. It is advisable to write your name, clearly, under your signature.

The style and tone of your letter will depend very much not only on the subject matter, but also upon your relationship with the recipient. Remember that a constructive but firm line will usually work better than a blustering or abusive tone, even when the letter is one of exasperated complaint.

39 Requesting service to central heating

(address and date)

Lincoln Gas
4 Dover Street
Lincoln LP4 6DG

Dear Sirs

We would like to have our central heating system serviced under the special 'parts only' plan advertised in the *Lincoln Post*. Our system is a Drayton 660.

(cont.)

There will be someone at home, each afternoon, after 2 pm.

Yours faithfully

A Barkworth

Similar letters can be used to request service to washing machines, televisions, etc. Stating the model number of the appliance in question can often mean quicker service.

---

40 To hotel/guest house, booking accommodation

(address and date)

The Manager
Sea View Hotel
The Promenade
Wadley Sands
Somerset SM3 1TX

Dear Sir

Further to our telephone booking of 15th March, this is to confirm that we would like a double room with sea view for six nights, arriving on 14th June and departing 20th June. We shall require full board.

I enclose a cheque for £20 deposit.

Yours faithfully

S M Parker

---

41 Excusing homework not done
(child to give to teacher)

(address and date)

Mr S Peterson
Berryford School
Berryford
Sussex SN3 4PD

Dear Mr Peterson

Juliet was unable to complete any homework last night because
she received rather a shining black eye playing hockey yesterday!
Although the swelling has gone down considerably today, she
found it very painful trying to read or concentrate yesterday
evening.

I hope she keeps her head down when next playing hockey!

Yours sincerely

Elizabeth Cooper (Mrs)

42 Excusing games

(address and date)

Miss R Simpson
Games Mistress
Berryford School
Berryford
Sussex SN3 4PD

Dear Miss Simpson

Please may I ask you to excuse Juliet from swimming for the
next few weeks.

(cont.)

She is suffering from a very nasty inner ear infection at present, and the doctor has told her she must not swim again until she has visited his surgery on 28th May to check that it has cleared up. Knowing what a keen swimmer she is, I would be grateful if you could make sure she doesn't sneak into the pool before that time.

Yours sincerely

Elizabeth Cooper (Mrs)

---

43 Putting a child's name down for preparatory school

(address and date)

Dr W R Weston
Headmaster's House
Shipley Court Preparatory School
Fawley Lane
Long Melford
Suffolk GU12 4ST

Dear Dr Weston

Our son Mark was born on the 28th June this year, and I am wasting no time in asking you to consider him as a boarding pupil for Shipley Court.

As you know, I was a pupil there myself, as was my father before me. I cannot think of a better preparation for life than that which is provided at Shipley Court, and it would give my wife and me great satisfaction to think that our son was to receive such fine educational and sporting opportunities.

We would prefer Mark to begin in the winter term following his 9th birthday and, of course, I should like him to join Askins, my old house.

My best wishes to Mrs Weston.

Yours sincerely

Peter M Hayward

---

44 Removing a child from school because of moving house

(address and date)

Miss M Metcalfe
Headmistress
Hampton Park School
Grazeley
Middlesex TW14 3RR

Dear Miss Metcalfe

I wish to inform you that our daughter, Rachel, will be leaving
Hampton Park at the end of this present term.

My husband's business has necessitated a move to Berkshire, and
Rachel will be attending Middle Hill School, just outside
Newbury which has, I understand, an excellent academic record.

Thank you for all the encouragement that you and your staff
have given to Rachel during the last two years.

Yours sincerely

Ester Walters (Mrs)

45 Excusing religious instruction

(address and date)

Miss S Butcher
Headmistress
Berryford School
Berryford
Sussex SN3 4PD

Dear Miss Butcher

Our son Sikandar is to be a pupil at your school at the start of
the winter term, and I am taking this opportunity to request that
he be excused from religious instruction.

(cont.)

Although he was born in this country, he has been raised in the Sikh faith, and receives instruction according to our own religion.

Yours sincerely

Dilip Patel

---

46 Moving a child from one school to another

(address and date)

Mr W Richardson
Headmaster
Brookfield School
Borsfield
Berkshire SL4 0AK

Dear Mr Richardson

I wish to inform you that our daughter, Carol, will be leaving Brookfield School at the end of next term.

Although she has only been at Brookfield for one term, it was always our hope that she would attend St Mary's School here in Oakleigh, since music is her great love, and is a subject greatly encouraged at that school. A place has now been made available.

I should like to say, however, that Carol has found Brookfield School an enjoyable place to study – even for so short a time – and has made many friends.

Yours sincerely

Simon Williams

---

47 Explaining a child's problem caused by bullying

(address and date)

Mr P Bowlson
Headmaster
Highfield Primary School
Dean Road
Bayford
Essex EP4 1SD

Dear Mr Bowlson

Our daughter Susan came home in tears last night. Apparently
she has been the victim of a group of older girls who pick on the
most junior pupils and demand money from them. When my
daughter refused to hand over the little money she had with her,
she was verbally abused and punched and kicked by several of
these older girls.

Susan does not tell tales, and can normally look after herself, but
this seems to be a particularly nasty form of bullying. She does
not know the names of the girls involved except one, Karen
Wilcox, who appears to be the ringleader.

As today is Friday, I am keeping Susan at home for the weekend.
She is still very upset, and quite badly bruised. I intend to
telephone you on Monday morning, when you will have
received this letter, to seek assurances from you that this bullying
will be nipped in the bud immediately and the culprits punished.

Yours sincerely

Carol Potter (Mrs)

48 To a purchaser regarding the sale of a house

(address and date)

Mr and Mrs S Boyer
16 Berry Close
Dunham
Bucks SB8 5SN

Dear Mr and Mrs Boyer

<u>32 Church Gardens</u>

I understand from our solicitors that all the arrangements both for the sale of the above property, and for our purchase of New Farm, are proceeding satisfactorily, and that exchange of contracts should take place at the beginning of August. Completion should then take place at the end of the third week in August.

As agreed, I am listing hereunder items that we are selling as 'fixtures and fittings', but which do not form part of the main contract.

> Brass door handles throughout;
> carpets and underlays in all downstairs
> rooms and hall, landing and stairs;
> lounge wall lights; roller blinds in kitchen
> and bathroom; curtains in master
> bedroom.............................. £550.00

Please make out a cheque in this sum payable to R. & J. Austin, and send it to our solicitors prior to completion.

Yours sincerely

Robin Austin

49   To an estate agent regarding the sale of a house

(address and date)

Miss M Wicks
Messrs Robinson Whitlow
19-21 High Street
Dunham
Bucks SB6 1BD

Dear Miss Wicks

32 Church Gardens, Dunham, Bucks

This is to confirm our agreement that your company will act as
sole agents for the sale of the above property at a commission
rate of 2% plus VAT. We understand that should we at any time
decide to offer the house for sale through joint agency, then the
commission rate due to your company will be 3% plus VAT
assuming your company introduces an eventual purchaser.

We further confirm that the sales particulars you have supplied
are satisfactory.

Yours sincerely

Robin Austin

50   To solicitors regarding the sale of a house

(address and date)

Messrs Upley, Pope and Dykes
5-7 Broad Street
Dunham
Bucks SB3 1BN

Dear Sirs

32 Church Gardens, Dunham, Bucks

(cont.)

This is to confirm our conversation of 14th May with Mrs Williams of your office, whereby we agreed to your partnership handling the conveyancing arrangements both for the sale of 32 Church Gardens, Dunham, Bucks, and the purchase of New Farm, Chilton Maltravers, Bucks. Your estimated fee was £950.00 plus VAT, stamp duty, land registration, searches and mortgage costs.

The purchasers of 32 Church Gardens are:

> Mr and Mrs S Boyer
> 16 Berry Close
> Dunham
> Bucks SB8 5SN

The vendors of New Farm are:

> Mr and Mrs R Chapman

Please let me know what further information you require in the form of mortgage account numbers, deeds, etc.

Yours faithfully

Robin Austin

---

51   To a builder requesting an estimate

(address and date)

Messrs Stokeley & Wicks
  (Builders) Ltd
46 Winlow Lane
Brackley
Lancs LN3 1ST

Dear Sirs

Would you please come and give us a written estimate for some alterations we wish to have carried out.

(cont.)

Basically the work entails removing an adjoining wall between two rooms, sealing up one doorway, and altering the position of one of the radiators and the light switch.

We would like to have the work carried out within the next three months. Please telephone us at any time to arrange a visit.

Yours faithfully

George Wills

Do not forget to include your telephone number where a supplier or business may wish to contact you by this method.

---

52 To a builder accepting an estimate

(address and date)

Messrs Stokely & Wicks   Your ref SW 63/GW
   (Builders) Ltd
46 Winlow Lane
Brackley
Lancs LN3 1ST

Dear Sirs

This letter is to confirm our acceptance of your estimate dated 4th October 19--.

We also confirm that a commencing date of 3rd November is satisfactory.

We look forward to seeing you at 9 am on that date.

Yours faithfully

George Wills

---

53 To a builder complaining about work carried out

(address and date)

Messrs Stokeley & Wicks   Your ref. SW 63/aw
    (Builders) Ltd
46 Winlow Lane
Brackley
Lancs LN3 1ST

Dear Sirs

You recently carried out some structural alterations and
redecoration at our house, but I have to tell you that the work
has proved to be most unsatisfactory.

Although initially all seemed to be fine, large cracks have
appeared throughout the new plasterwork on the ceiling.
Furthermore, moving the radiator has resulted in a constant
leakage from the union with the pipework. No amount of
tightening seems to cure this.

Will you please come and rectify these problems as soon as
possible since, apart from the unsightliness of the ceiling, it is
impossible to use the radiator at present.

Yours faithfully

George Wills

54   Objecting to environmental nuisance

(address and date)

The Environmental Health Officer
Copley Borough Council
Municipal Buildings
High Street
Copley
Sussex BN3 4PP

Dear Sir

I wish to complain about the early start being made by builders working on the flats in Spellthorne Park Road, which is only a few metres from our back garden.

For the last few days, work has commenced as early as 5 am! Since they are stacking and laying bricks, you can imagine the noise. Surely such an early start cannot be permitted, for it is almost impossible to sleep once they have begun.

I would be most grateful if you could look into this matter as soon as possible, to ensure that work begins at a more reasonable time.

Yours faithfully

S J Carter

The importance of such a letter is to bring the matter to the attention of the relevant body, who will then deal with it. The letter can be modified to cover poor roads, smells, etc. Look under the entry for Council in your telephone directory for the relevant body to contact.

55   Requesting a free sample of advertised goods

(address and date)

Castle Flooring Ltd
Dept DM 15
Queen Mary's Road
London NW6 3KT

Dear Sirs

Please send me a free sample of your 'No waste' floor covering. I enclose a stamped, self-addressed envelope.

Yours faithfully

N Chatterton

Enc.

There is no need to say in what publication you saw the advertisement. The letters and numbers in 'Dept DM 15' are the advertisers' own system of coding, telling them in which publication you read their advertisement.

56   Complaining about late delivery of goods

(address and date)

Countryways Fashion Wear Ltd
Countryways House
North Temple Street
Leeds LN6 1RR

Dear Sirs

On 16th September I sent you an order for a pair of 'Elegant Rider' ladies' fashion boots, together with a cheque for £42.00. These boots have not yet arrived and, since your advertisement states one should allow 28 days for delivery, I would be pleased if you would send my order immediately.

(cont.)

If there has been a delay in obtaining my size or preferred colours, it would have been a courtesy to inform me. Further, I know that my order has been received since my cheque has been cashed.

I look forward to either an explanation as to the delay, or my goods, by return of post.

Yours faithfully

Caroline Lockwood

---

57   Complaining about faulty goods (not returned)

(address and date)

Countryways Fashion Wear Ltd
Countryways House
North Temple Street
Leeds LN6 1RR

Dear Sirs

I recently received a pair of your 'Elegant Rider' ladies' fashion boots through mail order. However, I am afraid to say that they are faulty. Whilst one boot is perfect, the other has no stitching around the back of the heel. Since the heel support is glued and then stitched, the one on this particular boot would quickly pull away.

Shall I send the boots back to you for replacement, or do you have a local stockist to whom I may take them for replacement? If I return them to you, no doubt you will refund the cost of the postage and packing?

I look forward to your reply.

Yours faithfully

Caroline Lockwood

---

58 Complaining about fault goods (returned)

(address and date)

Graphic Toys Ltd
33-35 Eastdale Avenue
Shipton
Staffs SH1 1ZX

Dear Sirs

My son was recently given a Spacewriter kit for his birthday, which I enclose. As you can see, it has a manufacturing fault in the writing board, and in its present condition is unusable.

I would be grateful for a replacement or refund (including the cost of the postage for sending this item back to you) as soon as possible.

Yours faithfully

D Bull

Enc.

59 Stating change of address

(present address and date)

The Manager
Central Bank Limited
4 Market Street
Hartley
Ripon RR5 4BG

Dear Sir

Accounts Numbers: P & J Nayland, 1234567; J Nayland 98765434

Please note that from 29th May 19-- our new address will be:

(cont.)

16 Willmore Gardens,
Hartley
Ripon
RR6 7RG
(Telephone) Hartley 23186

Yours faithfully

Peter and Janet Nayland

---

60   To a tour operator complaining about accommodation

(address and date)

The Manager
Summer Tours Ltd
27 White Lane
Nottingham N3 7XC

Dear Sir

Holiday No. HO56; Receipt No. A1032

I am writing to complain about the accommodation provided for my wife and me from 11th to 24th August 19--.

I booked the above holiday at your offices on 16th February. At that time, I was told that we would be accommodated in an air-conditioned room with a balcony and private bathroom. This was confirmed in writing by Mr Jones on 20th February 19--, along with other details about the holiday. When we arrived at the hotel on 10th August we were shown to a room lacking all these amenities. We immediately pointed out the discrepancy to your courier, Alan Smith. After investigation, he informed us that the hotel had made a mistake over the booking and very much regretted that no other room was available.

(cont.)

The standard of accommodation which we were forced to accepted detracted considerably from our enjoyment of the holiday. Also, your company will have paid less for this room than for one of the advertised standard.

I, therefore, expect an appropriate rebate on the sum paid. I look forward to receiving this from you in the near future.

Yours faithfully

Robert Brown

---

61 Objecting to planning permission application

(address and date)

The Planning Officer
Brockford Council
Brockford Town Hall
218-240 Cross Road
Brockford
Cheshire C8 6FR

Dear Sir

Application for Planning Permission No. 1987

I wish to object to the proposed extension for which the above application has been made.

Having viewed the plans, I am sure that this building, if constructed, would block off the light from my lower rooms and much of my back garden during the afternoon and evening.

Therefore, I request that you reject this application.

Yours faithfully

R Hancock (Ms)

---

62   Reporting a dangerous road crossing

(address and date)

The Highways Department
Mossley Council
19-41 High Road
Mossley
Essex EX5 9SR

Dear Sirs

I wish to draw your attention to the pedestrian crossing on Cross Road, about 30 metres north of Cross Avenue. In my opinion, this crossing is a hazard.

Its siting, just over the brow of a hill, means that northbound traffic has insufficient warning of the crossing. The danger is increased after dark because overhanging trees virtually obliterate the light from the crossing beacons and surrounding lamp posts.

I drive along this stretch of road at least twice a day and have frequently witnessed narrowly averted accidents. I urge you to act promptly before a serious accident occurs.

I feel the crossing should be resited. Warning signs before the crossing would help, but I feel they would not eliminate the danger. In any event, the overhanging trees should be cut back immediately.

Please let me know as soon as possible what action you propose to take.

Yours faithfully

Anne Waters (Ms)

63 To a trading organisation regarding goods turning out to be faulty

(address and date)

The Manager
Comfort Home Furniture
51-53 High Road
Fairford
Essex ES9 7ES

Dear Sir

Receipt No. R635

I bought a sofa (Highfield, No. 87, Kingfisher) from your shop on 2nd April 19--. Although it has certainly not received more than normal wear and tear, it collapsed yesterday. It looks to me as if it is broken beyond repair.

I would be grateful if you would arrange for it to be taken away and inspected as soon as possible.

If you agree that it is irrepairable, I will require either an identical replacement or a refund.

I trust that you will give this matter your urgent attention.

Yours faithfully

David Miles

8. Business Matters

Business letters are, of course, almost as diverse as business itself. However, whether you are writing a letter enquiring about promotion prospects, or placing a large order with an overseas supplier, certain points should be borne in mind.

More than in any other type of letter, business letters must appear professional. They are your advertisement, and their presentation and construction reflect your own attitudes and ability. Try to write the sort of letter you would expect to receive in similar circumstances. It is not necessary to use 'long' words or slick phrases, but it is nevertheless true that business letters sometimes seem to have almost a language of their own, and so certain words and phrases which would appear out of place should be avoided.

Business letters frequently contain enclosures – other material sent at the same time. Your letter should state that enclosures are included, and you should ensure that they are enclosed. Remember, too, that business letters often include reference numbers or letters; quoting these when requested to not only saves the recipients' time, but also shows that you have read their letter correctly.

Company stationery will invariably have its own specially designed letter heading, but the recipient's name and address should normally appear on the left-hand side, even though the sender's name and address may, for instance, range across the top of the notepaper.

64 Asking for holiday entitlement

(department and date)

Mrs F Brown
Personnel Manager
Third Floor

Dear Mrs Brown

I would like to take two weeks of my holiday entitlement from 6-19th June inclusive, and the other two weeks from 9-22nd September inclusive.

I hope this is convenient.

Yours sincerely

Alan Jones

65 Asking for increased salary

(address and date)

Mr G Smith
Manager
Accounts Department
Basco Ltd
16-28 High Road
Cranton
Cheshire CH8 8HG

Dear Mr Smith

I write to ask whether you would consider reviewing my salary. Since my promotion two years ago, I have received no increase. Also, over the past few months, I have taken on additional responsibility. While I welcome this, I feel that it should be reflected in my remuneration.

(cont.)

I would be grateful for the opportunity to discuss this matter with you.

Yours sincerely

Barry Potter

If the letter is to be sent through an internal company post, you will only need to put your address within the company, e.g. Department A1. Similarly, the addressee's name, position and department will be sufficient.

If you do not wish the letter to be seen by anyone other than the addressee, put 'Private' or 'Personal' in the top left-hand corner of the envelope.

---

66 Apology for unforeseen absence

(address and date)

Mr G Smith
Production Supervisor
Jay Electronics Co. Ltd
28-34 Rompton Road
Leeds LS6 4VB

Dear Mr Smith

I regret that I was unable to return to work on 4th September. I reported for work on the 5th at the normal time.

Unfortunately, my holiday return flight from Majorca (Flight No. BS1084), which was due to depart at 1 pm on 3rd September, was delayed by adverse weather conditions. It eventually took off at 10 am on 4th September, and I arrived home at about 5 pm.

I am sorry for any inconvenience my absence may have caused.

Yours sincerely

Brian Jones

---

67   Asking for unpaid leave (compassionate)

(address and date)

Mr Nichols
Sales Manager
Grant & Sons Ltd
19 Church Lane
London SE4 9IG

Dear Mr Nichols

I would be grateful to receive permission to be absent from work next week (8-12th July).

I am needed to look after my mother, who is an invalid. The person who normally looks after her is required urgently elsewhere next week. At such short notice, I have been unable to arrange alternative care. This is an exceptional situation, which I do not anticipate will recur.

I hope that you will give my request sympathetic consideration. I appreciate that I would not be paid for the week.

Yours sincerely

Jane Ryman

If paid compassionate leave is anticipated, omit the last sentence.

68   Tendering resignation

(address and date)

Mr D Hobbis
Sales Manager
Creen & Sons Ltd
25 Weldon Road
Leeds LE1 8NM

Dear Mr Hobbis

I have been offered, and have decided to accept, the position of
Sales Manager with Broom & Sons Ltd. I am writing, therefore,
to give you the appropriate four weeks notice to terminate my
employment with the Company on 27th October.

I have been very happy during my five years here and it was
with some sorrow that I reached this decision. However, the new
position offers considerably more scope, responsibility and
security than my present one.

I would like to take this opportunity to thank you for all the
support and guidance you have given me over the past five
years.

Yours sincerely

Frank Rane

If you have not been happy in your employment, you may
want to omit the last two paragraphs.

69   Complaining about service

(address and date)

The Manager
Horns Ltd
23-37 Fairbridge Road
London EC1 3SD

Dear Sir

(cont.)

Invoice No. B512

I wish to complain about the standard of servicing offered by your Company, and about the above invoice.

I notified your Service Department on 20th June, in writing, that my washing machine needed repairing. Your service engineers have since been four times – on 11th July, 18th July, 26th July and 6th August. The fault was diagnosed on the first visit and the wrong replacement part was brought by different engineers on the two subsequent visits. The correct part was fitted by the original engineer on the fourth visit.

In summary, my complaints are:

1   I had to wait three weeks for an engineer to call and nearly two months for the machine to be repaired;

2   the engineers who called on 18th and 26th July had been given inadequate or wrong information by the Company, which resulted in my taking two half days off work unnecessarily;

3   the first and fourth visits lasted a total of 30 minutes. In the above invoice, I have been charged 4 hours labour for four visits. I do not intend to pay your Company for its mistakes. Indeed, I feel the Company should compensate me for the day's pay I lost through these mistakes.

Therefore, I shall not be paying the above invoice and look forward to receiving your response to these criticisms.

Yours faithfully

Robert Wallis

---

70   Making an appointment (general)

(address and date)

B. Boot Esq.
Boot Mather and Smith
12 City Chambers
London EC3 9ZX

Dear Mr Boot

I would like to make an appointment with you to discuss my will. Would the afternoon of Thursday 25th, or Friday 26th August, be convenient? I am most anxious to settle matters as quickly as possible.

Yours sincerely

Timothy Bright

71   Cancelling/postponing an appointment

(address and date)

B Boot Esq.   Your ref. BB/TB/92
Boot Mather and Smith
12 City Chambers
London EC3 9ZX

Dear Mr Boot

I am very sorry that I shall not be able to keep our appointment on Thursday 25th August. An urgent family matter has arisen which means I must be out of London until at least the end of the week.

I will telephone your secretary as soon as I return, to make an alternative arrangement.

I apologise for any inconvenience caused.

Yours sincerely

Timothy Bright

72 Asking for a season ticket loan

(address and date)

J Smith Esq.
Financial Director
Mace and Pole Limited
Tower Lane
London EC4 8JT

Dear Mr Smith

As you know, my journey into work is rather long and since the latest fares increase it is more costly than ever. Considerable savings can be made by purchasing an annual season ticket, and I wondered whether it would be possible for Mace and Pole to advance me the money to purchase one. The repayments could perhaps be deducted from my salary each month.

I would be most grateful if such an arrangement could be made.

Yours sincerely

Michael Firth

73 To a supplier requesting details of goods/ services

(address and date)

Champion Gates Limited
Furlong Road
Salhouse
Yorks RT7 6YN

Dear Sirs

I have seen your advertisement in *Gardening Weekly,* and I would be grateful for some further details about your wrought iron gates, as below:

(cont.)

1   Can you supply double gates to fit an opening 2.3 metres wide?
2   What type of gate posts do you recommend?
3   Can the gates be delivered, and if so at what charge?
4   Could you send me a brochure showing the styles you have available?

I look forward to your reply.
Yours faithfully

Thomas Crane

---

74   Apologising for the inability to supply goods/services

(address and date)

P Jones Esq.   Our ref. JPQ/7/92
Managing Director
Maxi Components Limited   Your ref. PJ/M/69
Lechford
Bucks SL8 9IV

Dear Sir

Thank you for your order of 28th June. Unfortunately we are no longer able to supply the black anodised aluminium you require, because of the introduction of new government safety regulations concerning the use of chemicals involved in the anodising process. May I refer you, however, to National Metallic Limited, Southfields Way, Broton, Yorks NW2 7DX, who import a similar product which does not infringe the Government safety regulations.

I apologise for this inconvenience, and hope that we may continue to supply your other aluminium requirements.

Yours faithfully
Marston Metal Supplies

Annette Wood

When writing letters in the course of your business, it is particularly important to put all the relevant information clearly and concisely, and to be polite at all times. State your appreciation of any order or letter to which you are replying, with its date. Set your requirements or answers out clearly, but avoid phrases such as 'thank you in advance', which preclude a refusal on the part of your correspondent. State your willingness to provide any further information needed, or your hope to be of further service to a customer.

75 Apologising for delay in supplying goods/ services

(address and date)

P Jones Esq.   Our ref. JPQ/7/92
Managing Director
Maxi Components Limited   Your ref. PJ/M/69
Lechford
Bucks SL8 9IV

Dear Mr Jones

Thank you for your order of 28th June. Unfortunately deliveries have been delayed slightly because of the rail strike, but your bolts will be dispatched to you as soon as possible. If you have not received them within two weeks, we would be grateful if you could notify us so that we can make alternative arrangements.

We appreciate your cooperation.

Yours sincerely
Marston Metal Supplies

Annette Wood

76 From a business apologising for a mistake

(address and date)

J Smith Esq.
Crown Paper Supplies
Fieldhouse Way
Longway
Bucks HY7 4RF

Dear Mr Smith

I must apologise most sincerely for our mistake in supplying you with white envelopes instead of the cream ones that you ordered.

I have today dispatched your correct order by special delivery, and I trust that it will have arrived by the time you receive this letter.

Please accept our regrets; I hope that we may continue to enjoy your valued custom.

Yours sincerely

Robert Adams
Managing Director

77 Circular letter (mailing shot) offering goods/ services

(address, phone number and date)

Dear

If you drive a car then we think we can help you.

With our up-to-the-minute equipment and a team of experienced motor engineers we can service your car to keep it in tip-top condition, and can carry out all engine and body work repairs.

MOT tests can be carried out while you wait, with no need to make an appointment.

If we need more than three days to repair your car we will supply you with another vehicle at highly competitive rates, and give you a full tank of petrol – FREE.

For your added convenience our engineers can come to your house and solve many of those annoying little problems without the need for you to go even outside your own front door.

So, if your car isn't quite perfect – or even if it is and you want to keep it that way – just pick up your 'phone – any of our staff will be delighted to help you.

Yours sincerely

James Brown
Managing Director

If a mailing shot is designed to look like a personal letter, take the trouble to find out the names of your potential clients, and fill in their names. Such letters should also be personally signed. A word processor is ideal for producing letters such as these.

9. Illness and Death

These can be among the most difficult letters to write, for obvious reasons. There is no need to dwell on the illness or death which may be the subject of your letter, although your letter should, of course, express the sympathy which is intended. Letters should normally be brief and to the point, and where they are personal and informal, handwritten. Where the illness is less serious, or where the writer of the letter is merely thanking the sender for good wishes or a gift, then a lighter, even humorous, approach is quite acceptable.

78 Condolences (informal)

(address and date)

Dearest Ruth

How grieved I was to hear of your father's death on Friday. It must have been a particularly bitter blow, since he seemed to be getting so much better.

There is so little one can say in these circumstances, but you know that Simon and I feel the loss very deeply, for he was like a second father to us.

I know that you are bound to be extremely busy for the next few days, so please may I come and help? I'm sure there's something I can do. I'll telephone you tomorrow, after you have received my letter.

All my love

Jane

This type of spontaneous letter has to 'come from the heart'. Don't force yourself on to a bereaved person at this time unless you really mean it.

79 Condolences (formal)

(address and date)

Dear Mrs Burroughs

I was deeply sorry to hear the news of Peter's sudden death last Tuesday. Please accept my sincerest condolences. I don't think I need to tell you how much he was respected and liked by everyone at the club. He will be greatly missed.

If there is anything that I can do to help in any way, you must not hesitate to ask.

With kindest regards

George Redman

80 Reply to a letter of condolence (formal)

(address and date)

Dear Mr Redman

Thank you very much for your kind thoughts and words. It gives me great comfort to know how highly everyone thought of Peter.

I appreciate, very much, your offer of help. Perhaps I may contact you, later.

With kindest regards

Wilma Burroughs

81   Sympathy on hearing of an illness (informal)

(address and date)

Dear Mary

I was very sorry to hear from John, when he got back from school, that Michael is ill. I do hope that it is not too serious and that he will be up and about again soon.

In the meantime, it would be no trouble for me to take Ruth and Anna to and from school with my own tribe and do your shopping and so on. If I can help in these or any other ways, please let me know.

John has asked me to send his best wishes to Michael.

With love from

June

82   Sympathy on hearing of an illness (formal)

(address and date)

Dear Mrs Brown

I was so sorry to learn of Mr Brown's accident. It must be a very trying time for you both. If there is anything that I can do to help either of you, I hope that you will not hesitate to contact me.

Please accept my sympathy and convey my best wishes for a speedy recovery to Mr Brown.

Yours truly

Jane Roberts

83 Sympathy regarding an invalid (likely to recover)

(address and date)

Dear Mr Patel

Please accept my sympathies during your wife's illness. I was relieved to hear that a diagnosis has been made and that she may well be on the road to recovery. This must have raised your spirits considerably.

I hope Mrs Patel will be up and about again soon. In the meantime, please give her my best wishes.

Yours sincerely

Ronald Grey

84 Sympathy regarding an invalid (not likely to recover)

(address and date)

Dear Mrs Smith

I was very sorry to hear that your husband has had to go into hospital again. It must be a very trying time, and my husband and I sympathise deeply with you both.

I know how busy you must be, but I hope you know that you are always welcome to drop in here at any time for a cup of tea and a chat. One or both of us is usually at home.

Yours truly

Anna Davies

85 Sympathy to an invalid (likely to recover)

(address and date)

Dear Uncle Bill

Jack and I have been very worried about you – it sounded as though you were having a tough time. I am so pleased you are now on the mend and that the doctors expect you to make a swift and complete recovery.

I was looking forward to seeing a bit more of you when we come up in April but, doubtless, by that time you will be back out on the golf course again!

Your loving niece

Rebecca

86 Sympathy to an invalid (not likely to recover)

(address and date)

Dear Mary

I was so sorry to learn of your illness. Your mother has told us how well you are taking everything, which is just what I would have expected. Your uncle and I have always been, and continue to be, very proud of you. We pray that you'll soon be on the mend and back home with the family before too long.

In the meantime, I do hope that we will be able to come down and see you sometime over the next few weeks. You are very much in our thoughts.

All my love

Aunt Ruth

Even though you know recovery is not likely, always offer hope to the invalid, and remember, a sick person may not be aware of just how ill he or she is; it would be disastrous for him or her to discover this from your letter of sympathy.

87   Thanks for sympathy on behalf of an invalid

(address and date)

Dear Michael

Thank you for your letter to John, which he enjoyed very much. Although he is not up to writing letters yet, his condition is improving steadily and he may be out of hospital in about a month.

In answer to your question, visiting times are 2 pm to 4 pm, and 6 pm to 8 pm every day. I am sure he would be delighted to see you if you found it possible to visit the hospital.

With best wishes

Emily Smith (Mrs)

88   Thanks for sympathy by an invalid

(address and date)

Dear Mr Jones

Thank you for your letter. It was so kind of you to think of me and very interesting to learn what has been going on at the Club during my absence.

I am feeling much better now and expect to be discharged sometime next week.

Please thank Mrs Jones for her good wishes which you conveyed.

Yours truly

Alan Brown

89 Excusing absence from work because of a relative's death

(address and date)

Mr C Smith
Personnel Officer,
Crane Co. Ltd.
48 Bridge Lane
Croxford
Lancs LA5 4DD

Dear Mr Smith

I regret that I was not a work today, 23rd September, and will be unable to attend for the rest of the week. My father died suddenly yesterday evening and I am needed back home in Lancashire to help settle his affairs and to make arrangements for the funeral. Also, all of us are very shaken by his death.

I expect to be back at work on Monday 29th September.

Yours sincerely

Carol Brown

90 Informing someone of a relative's death

(address and date)

Dear Mr Jones

I am very sorry to have to tell you that my brother died, thankfully peacefully, on Tuesday afternoon. Thank you for your many visits during his long illness. He was always in good spirits after seeing you.

The funeral will take place at Greenacre Crematorium, Church Lane, Ludlam, at 2 pm on 19th February.

Yours sincerely

Colin Smith

91 Formal letter of thanks for sympathies received following a death in the family

Mr S G Brown and family are grateful for the very kind messages of sympathy which they have received.

9th October 19--

> 64 Green Road
> London
> NW6 4SD

92 To an insurance company notifying them of a death

(address and date)

Trust Insurance Co Ltd
69 Croft Lane
London EC1 6DR

Dear Sirs

Trust Insurance Policy No. 6781

The holder of the above policy, Gerald Young, died on 28th June. I enclose a copy of the Death Certificate.

I am executor of his will. I shall need to know the amount of money the beneficiary will receive, and when. Also, confirmation is required that the deceased's widow, Mrs Gloria Mary Young, is still the named beneficiary.

Please let me know if you need further documents before sending me these details.

Yours faithfully

Andrew Blake

Enc.

10. Landlord and Tenant

When there is a query or dispute between a landlord and his tenant, it is wise for both parties to put their point of view formally in a letter. If the letters are clearly written they may themselves help to clear up any misunderstandings, and an amicable solution be facilitated. If the problem is more deep-seated, it is possible that legal steps may follow from one side or the other, and if this happens it will be much quicker and cheaper for everybody concerned if the points of view have been clearly stated in writing at an early stage, and copies kept of all letters sent.

Just as for any other business letter, make sure that you acknowledge any letter you are answering, and reply to the questions it raised. State all the relevant facts and put your points firmly, but whatever your feelings may be it will never be helpful to become abusive – indeed, written abuse can lead to serious trouble.

You should note that landlord and tenant regulations are very subject to change. You would do well to seek guidance and information from a Citizens' Advice Bureau *before* you make any approach to an official body such as The Rent Officer, The Rent Assessment Committee or The Rent Tribunal, on any landlord/tenant problem. The Citizens' Advice Bureau will be able to advise you of current legislation and to whom you should (or should not) write with your problem. If your query is a straightforward one, it is suggested that you telephone for an appointment so that the right person is available to help you. If your query is more complex, it would be better to write a short letter.

93 To a Citizens' Advice Bureau about a possible rent rebate

(address and date)

Citizens' Advice Bureau
2 Queen Street
Blessop
Lincs LR4 8AB

Dear Sirs

I rent a two-bedroomed house at the address above, through
House Providers Ltd of Covchester. My take-home pay is, at most,
£180 per week. Our weekly rent has just been increased to £48
per week. With three small children and another on the way, I am
finding it hard to cope. A colleague suggested I tried for a rent
rebate, but I have no idea how to go about applying, and to whom.

Could I please make an appointment to talk things over with one
of your Advisors. Any lunchtime between noon and 2 p.m.
would be most convenient, if this is possible. I enclose a stamped
addressed envelope.

Yours faithfully

John Collins

94 To a Citizens' Advice Bureau about unfair rent

(address and date)

Citizens' Advice Bureau
2 Queen Street
Blessop
Lancs LR4 8AB

Dear Sirs

Confirming our telephone conversation this morning, I shall be
pleased to speak to your advisor at 10 a.m. on Monday 6 April.

I am sure I am being asked for a very unfair rent for this
property which is in an extremely poor state of repair and will be
very grateful for any advice you can offer me as to what action I
should take.

Yours faithfully

Mary Stopps (Mrs)

95 To the agent about early reoccupation

(address and date)

Mr Brian Buckland
Buckland Ballard and Partners
15 New Street
London SW1 5PJ

Dear Brian Buckland

4 Stanswick Road

Thank you for your letter of 3rd July concerning the tenancy of 4 Stanswick Road. I would like new tenants found as soon as possible since, as you know, the financial loss and the risk involved in having an empty property is considerable.

Yours sincerely

Michael Brown

96 To the agent concerning repairs

(address and date)

Mr Brian Buckland
Buckland Ballard and Partners
15 New Street
London SW1 5PJ

Dear Brian Buckland

Thank you for your letter of 3rd July regarding repairs to Nos 4 and 6 Stanswick Road.

Both roofs must of course be made good. Would you please obtain three estimates and forward them to me for consideration.

(cont.)

The request for a new sink unit in the kitchen of No. 4 worries me a little. I see from my records that a new sink was installed only four years ago, for the same tenants. Could you visit the house and inspect the general condition in which the tenants are maintaining the property? I would appreciate your recommendation on the matter.

I shall be on holiday for four weeks from 10th August, and would like to settle all these matters before I go.

Yours sincerely

Michael Brown

---

97 To a housing advice centre about unfair eviction

(address and date)

The Blessop Housing Advice Centre
Orion Precinct
Blessop
Lancs UP8 6TG

Dear Sirs

I would be grateful if you could tell me whether it is legal for a landlord to evict me despite the fact that I pay the rent regularly.

I have been renting a partly-furnished two-bedroomed flat at the above address for just over five years, during which time I have only once been in arrears with the rent. For the past year the rent has been £65 per week and I have paid this sum to my landlord in person each week.

On 16th August my landlord told me that he needed my flat for his brother-in-law's use. He gave me notice to leave by 15th September. I have told him that I cannot find alternative accommodation and that I will not leave. Yesterday he came to say that the builders will be arriving on 6th September to redecorate the flat for his brother-in-law.

(cont.)

I cannot possibly find another suitable flat at such short notice and would therefore much appreciate your advice as to my legal position.

Yours faithfully

Stuart Hall

---

98   From a landlord to a tenant requesting overdue rent

(address and date)

Mr P Smith
94 Court Road
Poolford
Dorset JO9 5TB

Dear Mr Smith

I am afraid I must remind you again that the rent due on 30th April for the property you occupy at 94 Court Road, has still not been received.

Unless full payment is made within seven days of the date of this letter I shall be forced to put the matter into the hands of my solicitor.

Yours sincerely

Ian Graham

---

99 Reply to a landlord requesting overdue rent

(address and date)

I Graham Esq.
40 Moreley Drive
Poolford
Dorset JP8 6YB

Dear Mr Graham

Thank you for your letter of the 3rd June. I am very sorry that you have had to write to me requesting payment of my rent, which I know is overdue.

The last three months have been very difficult for me since I was made redundant. However, I have now started work again and with a regular wage I will try to pay off my debt to you as quickly as possible. Would you agree to my paying an extra £5 per week until the backlog is cleared?

I realise now that I should have explained the situation to you sooner, and hope that you will accept my apologies.

Yours sincerely

Peter Smith

100 To a landlord concerning recurring repairs

(address and date)

I Graham Esq.
40 Moreley Drive
Poolford
Dorset JP8 6YB

Dear Mr Graham

I am afraid I must inform you that the window in our kitchen still cannot be opened more than a couple of inches, despite the efforts of your workmen on 6th May.   (cont.)

I would very much appreciate it if you could arrange a further attempt to be made to free it. As I am sure you will understand, my wife has been finding her kitchen less than fresh during the recent hot weather.

With many thanks for your attention in this matter.

Yours sincerely

Peter Smith

If you normally think in metric terms, by all means use 'about five centimetres' instead of 'a couple of inches'.

---

101 To a landlord concerning repairs (stronger in tone)

(address and date)

I Graham Esq.
40 Moreley Drive
Poolford
Dorset JP8 6YB

Dear Mr Graham

Kitchen at 94 Court Road

I am afraid that I feel I must write to you again about the state of our kitchen.

We received a visit from your building contractor, Mr Ady, on 14th May, when he promised to bring a new sink unit within one week. He also promised to repair the window the following day. Neither of these things has happened.

As you know, the sink unit was cracked to the extent of being unusable when we moved here on 1st April. The window has been attended to once already, but clearly without success since we are still unable to open it more than an inch or two.

(cont.)

The hot weather recently has made the almost unventilated kitchen extremely unpleasant for my wife and children, and my wife is finding life very difficult in having only the use of the washbasin in the bathroom.

I would appreciate your immediate attention to these matters.

Yours sincerely

Peter Smith

However justifiably angry you may feel, never threaten legal action or the involvement of sanitary inspectors or the like unless you really intend to carry out your threat.

---

102 From a landlord refusing to make improvements

(address and date)

Mr P Smith
94 Court Road
Poolford
Dorset JO9 5TB

Dear Mr Smith

Thank you for your letter of 1st August, requesting the installation of double glazing in your bathroom and kitchen. I am afraid, however, that it is quite impossible for me to consider paying for any such major improvements for some time.

During the last two years most of the rent has been absorbed by the various repairs and redecoration work, and the property has become a severe drain on my own income.

While I do not wish to seem unreasonable, I am forced to refuse your request.

Yours sincerely

Ian Graham

---

103   From a tenant asking for an extention of time to pay the rent

(address and date)

I Graham Esq.
40 Moreley Drive
Poolford
Dorset JP8 6YB

Dear Mr Graham

I write to ask whether you would be kind enough to allow me an extension of time in which to pay my rent?

I recently suffered an accident which has meant that I have been away from work for six weeks. As a result I have been very short of money. I am returning to work on Monday 20th May and will therefore soon be able to get my finances on a sound footing once more. I would be most grateful if you could agree to my paying this month's rent in two instalments at the ends of June and July.

Yours sincerely

Peter Smith

104   From a tenant concerned about defects in the house he is occupying

(address and date)

Mr I Graham
40 Moreley Drive
Poolford
Dorset JP8 6YB

Dear Mr Graham

I wish to inform you of my concern at the dampness in the property I rent from you at 94 Court Road.

(cont.)

Throughout last winter we found it almost impossible to rid the house of its musty smell. Clothes and bedlinen were always slightly damp when taken out of cupboards or drawers; those kept in the fitted bedroom cupboard at the rear of the house were worst affected. My anxieties have increased since discovering two damp patches on the dining room wall.

I would much appreciate it if you could send a builder to assess the situation as soon as possible. It would, of course, be more pleasant for my family and more beneficial to the property if any necesssary work could be carried out before the onset of another winter.

I will be most grateful for your early attention to this matter.

Yours sincerely

Peter Smith

TO HODGES & SONS ELECTRICIANS...

11. Money Matters

Letters about money matters should always be written in the clearest and most precise manner possible. It is best to avoid archaic phrases which your reader may misunderstand, and to write in concise sentences which leave no possibility of ambiguity.

When writing letters to a firm or financial institution it is best to address a particular individual. If you cannot find out the name of the appropriate person, at least make sure that your letter goes to the correct department. Within large organisations, and some smaller ones too, it can take some time for a letter to arrive on the desk of the person who can deal with it if it arrives in the post room bearing no name.

Just as with any non-personal letter, those concerning money should always be polite – even if you are angry. State the subject matter of the letter in your first paragraph, and follow through the other points you want to make in a logical order. By sticking entirely to the facts in this way, you will put your case with the least likelihood of misunderstanding or offence.

Quite often it may be helpful to enclose relevant documents such as receipts. If you do this, send copies, not the originals, and say what you have enclosed in the text of your letter. To avoid any possible difficulties at a later stage it is wise to keep a copy of any letter you write on a financial matter.

Always quote any reference given on a letter to which you are replying. Even if you do not use references yourself, they will help your fellow correspondent and thus speed up the handling of your business.

105   Asking for a bill to be paid

(address and date)

E Wolverton Esq.   our ref. ABC/JS/9
63 West Street
London NW10 9PD

Dear Sir

A statement of your account with this company was sent to you
on 16th December 19--. Since we have not yet received your
remittance for the amount due, it is possible that our letter was
mislaid in the post.

We would appreciate it if you could confirm that you have not
received our statement so that we can supply a copy. If you have,
in fact, received our statement, we would be grateful for
settlement of the outstanding sum.

Yours faithfully
Frank Acton and Company

John Smith
Accounts Manager

106   Pressing for a bill to be paid

(address and date)

E Wolverton Esq.   Our ref. ABC/JS/9
63 West Street
London NW10 9PD

Dear Sir

We much regret having to call your attention to the account we
sent to you on 16th December 19--. Having written to you on
22nd January 19-- in case the original statement had been
mislaid, we can only conclude that our requests are being
wilfully ignored.

(cont.)

Payment is now long overdue, and we must ask that you settle the outstanding debt of £178.64 by return of post.

Yours faithfully
Frank Acton and Company

John Smith
Accounts Manager

---

107   Requesting settlement of an account

(address and date)

F Hunter Esq.   Our ref. NT/92
63 Westerham Road
Broughton
Sussex LU9 6TV

Dear Sir

We would much appreciate your payment for the timber supplied to you during October and November 19--.

We are now preparing our books for auditing and the delay in receiving your settlement is causing some inconvenience.

A duplicate statement is enclosed.

Yours faithfully
Napley Timber Limited

Brian Kent

Enc. 1 sheet

---

108   Replying to a creditor

(address and date)

P Harvey Esq.
Managing Director
Napley Timber Limited
Walter's Yard
Broughton
Sussex LU7 5TN

Your ref. NT/92

Dear Mr Harvey

I have this morning received your warning of legal proceedings in connection with my outstanding account. I am extremely sorry that you should feel such a step necessary, and no less sorry that I should have been the cause of it.

Since I have been a customer of yours for more than five years, and have settled my account promptly each month throughout that time, I trust that you may reconsider the matter. I have to admit that my finances have been strained recently, due to various unexpected extra costs. However, I confidently expect to return to a more solid basis next month and would be happy to issue a promissory note for the sum involved plus any reasonable interest.

I hope that you will accept this offer, and my apologies for the inconvenience I have caused.

Yours sincerely

Frank Hunter

When requesting a business favour this more personal style of letter can be successfully used. However, it should be used with caution if you do not know your correspondent personally, since it could appear presumptuous.

109   Complaining of an overcharge in an invoice

(address and date)

Accounts Department
Sportsman's Aid Limited
Sporting House
Myers Industrial Estate
Ludley
Wiltshire YT7 4XT

Dear Sirs

I have this morning received your invoice dated 25th November. As you will see, the second item is for two dozen X6 golf balls, at a total cost of £48. These were on my original order, but cancelled in writing on 15th November. I must assume that you received this cancellation, since the balls were not included in my delivery.

I am returning your invoice and when it has been amended I shall be pleased to send you my cheque.

Yours faithfully

Michael Garfield

Enc. 1 sheet

Do not forget to enclose the invoice.

110   Promissory note

(address and date)

£246
Three months after date, I promise to pay Napley Timber Limited, or order, the sum of Two Hundred and Forty Six pounds sterling for value received.

Frank Hunter

111 To a bank confirming that a cheque should be stopped

(address and date)

The Manager
London and District Bank
119 Bolton Street
Royburn
Berkshire YN6 5FV

Dear Sir

Account No. 8181812 S.F. Dennis

This is to confirm my telephone call of this morning asking you to stop payment of my cheque, number 4248 638, dated 4th July 19--. It was for the sum of £586 and was signed by me in favour of Mr Eric Palfrey.

Mr Palfrey has not received the cheque and I must therefore assume that it has been lost in the post.

Yours faithfully

Simon Dennis

Only stop a cheque for a good reason, such as that it has been lost or that fraud is suspected. You will have to pay the bank for stopping a cheque.

112 Confirming the loss of a cheque card

(address and date)

E R Cox Esq.
The Manager
London and District Bank
119 Bolton Street
Royburn
Berkshire YN6 5FV

Dear Mr Cox

Account No. 8181812 S.F. Dennis

(cont.)

I write to confirm my telephone call of this morning, in which I informed a member of your staff, Miss Jones, that I have lost my cheque card, Number 456789.

I first noticed the loss of my card this morning, and I know that it was in my wallet on 8th May when I used it to cash my cheque, number 4248 701 at your High Street branch.

Yours sincerely

Simon Dennis

---

113 To a bank concerning a temporarily overdrawn account

(address and date)

E R Cox Esq.
The Manager
London and District Bank
119 Bolton Street
Royburn
Berkshire YN6 5FV

Dear Sir

It will have come to your notice that my account (number 5537–642) has been marginally overdrawn on four occasions in the last two months. With the winter fuel bills due to be paid soon, I am afraid that this will happen again, and I would be grateful if you could let me have proper overdraft facilities up to £500. I would expect to need such an arrangement until the end of this July when my salary increase should enable me to repay the debt.

I would of course be quite willing to come in and discuss the matter with you should you think it necessary.

Yours faithfully

Sylvia Black

---

114 To a building society advising them of difficulty in paying mortgage because of redundancy

(address and date)

The Manager
Midlands Building Society
Abbey House
Upper High Road
Gloster
Oxon LM8 9AB

Dear Sir

Mortgage policy number 898/LMR/63

I am afraid I must write to inform you that I am having considerable difficulty in meeting my mortgage repayments, and can foresee no immediate improvement in my financial situation.

My employers for the last fifteen years, J.M. Smith and Company, went into liquidation in January and I was therefore made redundant. I am of course actively seeking another position, but as you will appreciate employment is not easy to find at present in this area.

I have some savings in addition to my redundancy payment, but despite cutting back on many fronts I am finding it hard to meet all my commitments. It would cause great upset for my family if we were forced to give up the house, and I wondered therefore if I might be allowed to reduce my monthly payments by 20% for the present, extending the total length of my mortgage to compensate for this? After careful consideration I am certain that I could meet the interest payment regularly, and I very much hope that you will give your sympathetic consideration to my situation.

I would naturally be happy to come and discuss this matter further with you, if you feel it would be helpful.

Yours faithfully

Malcolm Jones

115 To a building society advising of difficulty in mortgage payment because of the death of husband/wife

(address and date)

The Manager
Midlands Building Society
Abbey House
Upper High Road
Gloster
Oxon LM8 9AB

Dear Sir

Mortgage policy number 898/LMR/63

I am sorry to inform you that my husband, Mr Malcolm Jones, in whose name the above mortgage was held, died on 6th December.

I have not yet sorted out his financial affairs, but I know that he did not have a mortgage protection policy. I believe that his life assurance policy and my widow's pension will enable me to meet the mortgage payments in the future, but I fear that I will have some difficulty in finding the funds for the next three payments or so. I wonder if it would be possible for my next three payments to be deferred and the length of the mortgage extended accordingly?

I would much appreciate your understanding at this difficult time.

Yours faithfully

Gladys Jones

116 To a hire purchase company advising of difficulty in meeting repayments

(address and date)

Southern Credit Company
12-14 Arlington Street
London SW1 6HL

Agreement HP23/64/82

I am having some difficulty in meeting the repayments for the car that I am buying in accordance with the terms of the above agreement. The contract was signed on 12th August 19--, and since then I have paid regularly each month. Unfortunately I now find that my commitments are more than my financial situation will stand.

I have no wish to default on my debt to your company, and would therefore much appreciate it if you would consider allowing me to make rather smaller payments over a longer period.

I would be most grateful if you could let me know whether such an arrangement is possible and, if so, what terms you are able to offer.

Yours faithfully

Peter Smithson

As with any debt about which there is some difficulty, it is advisable to write to the creditor and make whatever realistic offer you can.

117   To an insurance company advising of a theft

(address and date)

Reliant Insurance Company Limited
Pimlico Street
London SW1 6XJ

Dear Sirs

Policy Number LM 169380

I have to report that a theft occurred at the above address on the
night of 19th May 19--.

My wife and I were both at home on the night in question, but
knew nothing of the theft until 7.30 am on the morning of 20th
May, when I realised that the kitchen window was open. We
quickly discovered that various items were missing, and
telephoned the police. I have made a full statement to the police
at Banwood Police Station, where Detective Inspector Charles is
in charge of the case.

I enclose a full list of the items that are missing, with their
replacement values. Fortunately, nothing irreplaceable was taken
and I have been able to confirm the values quite easily.

I will willingly give you any further information that may be
helpful, and hope that a settlement can be made without delay.

Yours faithfully

Barry Spinks

Enc. 1 sheet

Always inform your insurance company of any claim
immediately, even if you do not yet know the extent of the
loss. Most companies will then send you a claim form to fill in,
which would take the place of the list sent with the above
letter.

118 To an insurance company in respect of a car accident when you believe it was your fault

(address and date)

Resteasy Insurance Company
Resteasy House
Lutton
Surrey FT5 7YB

Dear Sirs

Policy Number 685 LM 982 Z

I have to report that this afternoon, whilst driving down Maida Vale, I was involved in an accident with a car when I was turning right into Boundary Road. Thankfully, no one was injured.

My own car has suffered severe denting to the offside wing, which I believe will have to be replaced. The other car will require new head and side lights, a new front bumper and some repairs to the paintwork.

The driver of the other car (registration number RNP 852P) is Mr John Bolton of 15 Harp Gardens, London, NW3 7TX. He is insured with the Kingly Insurance Company. We were not able to obtain the names of any witnesses to the accident.

I would be grateful if you could send me the necessary claim forms which I will complete and return to you as soon as I have an estimate for the repairs from my garage.

Yours faithfully

James Sudbury

Never give the go ahead for repairs to start before getting the estimate(s) approved by your insurance company. It is wise not to admit liability at this stage. You will be asked, on your claim form, to state who was responsible for the accident.

119 To an insurance company in respect of a car accident when you believe it was not your fault

(address and date)

Resteasy Insurance Company
Resteasy House
Lutton
Surrey FT5 7YB

Dear Sirs

Policy Number 685 LM 982 Z

I have to report that this evening, whilst I was driving down Maida Vale, a van overtook me and severely scraped the side of my car.

The accident was, on his own admission, entirely the fault of the other driver. His name is Ian Morton and he is an employee of Coast Deliveries (6 Oak Court, London SE16 2XN) whose van he was driving at the time. Since no one was injured in any way, and the cause of the accident is not in dispute, the police were not called. However, a Mrs Ann Wood, of 16 Arley Road, London N8 4SP, saw the incident clearly and has given me permission to mention her name should an independent witness be called for.

I have not yet obtained estimates for the repairs needed, but will forward them to you in the next few days. In the meantime, would you please send me the necessary claims forms.

Yours faithfully

James Sudbury

If an accident was not your fault, make certain to keep your no claims bonus.

Index of Example Letters

INVITATIONS AND REPLIES

LOVE, COURTSHIP, MARRIAGE & FAMILY

APPOINTMENTS

DOMESTIC MATTERS

BUSINESS MATTERS

ILLNESS AND DEATH

LANDLORD AND TENANT

MONEY MATTERS

Opening doors to the World of books

Book Tokens

Book Tokens can be bought and exchanged at most bookshops